The *Church* Made WHOLE:

Healing For Your Body, The Church Body, And The Whole Body of Christ

By
Deidre Campbell-Jones

Destination Publications

ALSO BY DEIDRE CAMPBELL-JONES:

Be Made Perfectly Whole:
Body, Spirit & Soul

© 2018 – Destination Publications
DestinationChristianBooks.com
Sylmar, CA 91342

ISBN-10: 1-892939-03-7
ISBN-13: 978-1-892939-036
First Edition – Printed in the United States of America

Written by Deidre Campbell-Jones
Cover photo by Terrance C. Jones

**Dedicated to me,
and to the Church I pastor:
The House of His Glory
Sylmar, CA**

*This project was a labor of obedience
and a lesson in divine partnership.*

*I have learned that delayed obedience
is not the same as disobedience –
but instead it is a catalyst for delayed blessings.*

*My prayer is for the immediately, suddenly, in that
self-same hour, supernatural blessings of
divine health, healing, power and glory,
to my body; the church body; to your body;
and the whole body of Christ.*

CONTENTS

1

Wellness

∽Church Life

Workbook Question: Is Your Church Living or Dying?

I believe the church as a whole – the church universal – is a macrocosm of the individual Believer. And that each individual church is a collective reflection of the health, growth and physical well-being of the individuals that make up their congregational membership.

Churches are its own living, breathing entity. A Church has life. It is a life that exists because the Church is made up of the lives of Christians. We know that a new, baby church plant (just like a new born Christian) must grow and mature in its ministry, and unfortunately we know of far too many churches that have died as well. And just like the individuals that make up the church that dies, it is more likely to be a death that is untimely and unexpected instead of from "natural causes." In fact, there really is no such thing in relation to the death of a church. And even a church that dies peacefully in its sleep from "old age" is not a death that is somehow more desirable.

Death, whether of a church or a person is the last enemy of God[1] and not a part of the abundant and everlasting life He intends for everyone who comes to the knowledge of Jesus.

Like each new Believer that comes to Christ and receives eternal life through their salvation; God has everlasting life in mind for the Church – the Church who is the Bride of His son Jesus. This church will be one that Jesus will present to Himself, a glorious church without spot, blemish or wrinkle.[2]

Say that again!

God has everlasting life in mind for the Church – Forever as the Bride of Christ!

And we will be presented to Jesus: a glorious Bride without spot, blemish or wrinkle!

But if we were to take a look at the worldwide Christian Church today, we would see a Bride who is sick, weak, old and blemished with many shameful, even ugly spots and wrinkles. We see the same illnesses of the world reflected throughout local congregations and, over the years, denominations that were once strong and healthy are now diseased and dying.

❧Church Revelation

Workbook Question: Is Your Church Maturing?

Overall if we were to look at the most significant spiritual and biblical revelations of Jesus in the Church throughout church history, we can see them as stages of growth within the Church.   These historical revelations then, become a reflection of Church growth that is much like, and very similar to the stages of growth and maturity that an individual person goes through as well.

But unlike the growth of a person that is physical, emotional and intellectual unto the culmination of death; conversely the church's physical, emotional and spiritual growth over time should be a maturation that comes revelation by revelation, that will ultimately bring life and unity within the church body and begin – without end – at the return of Jesus.

Ephesians 4:13
"Till we all come in the unity of the faith, and of the knowledge of the Son of God, unto a perfect man, unto the measure of the stature of the fullness of Christ:"

When looking at historical periods of revelation to the church such as the Reformation Era, or revivalist movements, we must see that when the church learned salvation is by faith, that fresh, revelatory knowledge at that time, wasn't cancelled out by learning that by faith we live under grace and not law - in the same manner that a baby's ability to crawl is not cancelled out and made false or in error when the toddler learns to walk.

Therefore, since Jesus has not yet returned, the church is not through maturing. And NEW revelations of the word of God and its application to our lives are still being revealed for the maturing of the individual (and ultimately the whole church) who understands and walks in each new truth.

Also, it must be clarified that these "new truths" are not new to God or His written word! Instead, they are new to us – newly revealed and newly applied scriptural truths. Isaiah 45:2 says, "Behold, I will do a new thing in you." Each new thing that is new to those of us who hear it, will not be received by all. They do not recognize "new" as being of God because it does not match their "old" understanding of the Word.

Biblically, new revelations should not cancel out old ones. Historically however, new revelations are usually not easily received – they are rejected, rebuked, criticized and disparaged. However, those revelations that are truly of God will prevail through the religious rebuff. But like most children who learn anything new it may be learned incorrectly and will need to be corrected for continued and proper development.

Babies will scooch instead of crawl; toddlers will walk and bounce on their toes instead of starting from their heels and young children will mispronounce their words. Sometimes, as adults we think these things are cute, or that the child will grow out of them naturally – not realizing the harm that might come later. Babies that skip learning to crawl before walking, could have learning disabilities – especially in the areas of math.[3] Toddlers that walk on their toes may not develop their tendons properly and need corrective surgery later.[4] And kids who consistently form certain words incorrectly may develop severe speech impediments that persist into adulthood.[5]

The church is the same way. There have been revelations learned by individuals and churches that have been learned incorrectly, or that have been distorted, abused or twisted to the degree that now the universal understanding of those revelations has become detrimental to the maturity, growth and physical stability of the overall church.

While many of these revelations may now need corrective surgery, they were not wrong in their original understanding. These revelations – the ones given by the Spirit of Truth - are still necessary to the maturation of the church and for the benefit of the individual Christian.

CHURCH NOTE:

Don't throw the baby out with the bath water! Be bold and even brave enough to go back and revisit "old beliefs." Study the word of God and ask the Spirit of Truth within you for new revelation of His word and a fresh vision of His desires for your congregation.

ᴓChurch Epidemic

Workbook Question: Is Your Church "Normal?"

The church generation today is now experiencing wide spread spiritual detriment and false understandings that are both accepted as "common" or even "normal" – in the same way that our children are now widely diagnosed with ADHD and Juvenile Diabetes.

We have made wrong choices in the foods we've exposed our children to but didn't know they were wrong or altered or potentially dangerous, especially when we thought we were doing right. Likewise the enemy has infiltrated the revelations of God to the church and warped what we have been fed spiritually in a way that we did not recognize as being wrong, altered or potentially dangerous.

In the recent past, it was time for the teen-aged church to learn new revelations regarding faith. But extreme abuses and miss-applications of these truths produced a church-wide epidemic of thought that has been similar to the epidemic of teen-aged pregnancy.

Only God creates life and yet there is still a "wrongness" to teenaged pregnancy. But society has seemingly lost its battle with this issue to such an extent that now there are reality shows that seem to support and vilify the issue. Such is the case with faith. God gave the revelation but there is now a "wrongness" in the way the church has been excessive with it.

Puberty is not the source of teenaged pregnancy any more than Mark 11:22-24 is the source of the "Name it & Claim it" philosophy. Puberty is necessary for an individual to grow and mature into a procreating adult that is physically able to further the human race. Faith in God and the ability to believe that what you say will come to pass and do not doubt in your heart, is necessary for the church to grow and mature into a replicating ecclesia, able to walk in multiplication blessing and re-create the Kingdom of God in every environment in Earth. [6]

Today, teens in the world are exposed to television programs and commercials; movies; songs; digital gaming, social media and peer perpetuated philosophies that promote and glorify a drug using; sexually explicit and exploited; gender confused, violent and angry counter-culture. Then in response to the adverse consequences of their widely accepted life-styles, they are given a cocktail of Band-Aid type "solutions" like abortions, HPV vaccinations and gender-neutral restrooms.

But this is where the analogy of the church compared to teenaged pregnancy and sexuality begin to diverge. The world would like to see the now teen-aged Church die of its own immune deficiency disorder – as the church is widely unable to remain immune to the same physical and emotional maladies, disorders and diseases as the world.

Christians have homosexual and gender confused kids and the churches they belong to are ill-equipped to teach, rebuke[7] and help them with Truth, love and no condemnation.

Christians live in a world of debt, poverty, lack and financial hardships and many of their churches will invite financial advisors from their own congregations (many of whom struggle with the same financial issues), to teach them the economic solutions offered by the world instead of relying on the truth of God's Kingdom Economics by faith.

And most of all, Christians are dying from a long list physical ailments such as Cancer; Diabetes; Lupus; Leukemia; Hypertension and Heart Disease. They suffer in constant pain from Crohn's Disease; Migraines; Arthritis and a host of back issues and muscle spasms. And Believers in every church struggle horribly with the same Irritable Bowell Syndrome; Infertility; Asthma; Incontinence; stress, depressions and various addictions as the rest of the world.

And the same world that has accepted these problems and then manufactured their own solutions for them (many of which cause more problems), will not offer up any vaccines or inoculations to prolong the life, health and well-being of the Church, in fact, exactly the opposite.

In the New Testament, the word "witchcraft" is used once (Gal. 5:20). In the Greek, this word is "pharmakeia" (from which we get our words pharmacy and pharmaceutical). It means: medication; magic or sorcery; a drug or spell giving potion. And in the Greek, a Pharmacist is defined as a poisoner! This is what the world offers as solutions to every disease, pain, illness, headache, sickness, stress-related and infertility issues!

And as the church body suffers from the same problems as the world; they also seek the same solutions as, commiserate with, and stand in agreement with the same world that would rather see the church remain sterile and infertile or at least, only reproduce sickly, diseased, religiously-spiritual children with short, ineffective lives that are no threat to their own.

Truthfully, the Church is intended by God to have the solutions to all of these problems and more – not just for themselves, but for the world!

Say that again!

God has intended for the Church to have the solutions to all the problems of the world - not just for themselves but also for the world!

With an understanding of the Word of God and the Law of the Spirit of Life that quickens our mortal bodies, (Romans 8:2 & 11), the Church can live in divine health, wholeness and a well-being that will not only provoke the world to jealousy and good-works but also be the best witness of Christ in our lives and the best evangelistic tool for reaching the lost with the true love of Christ.

The Church should be walking in the kind of revelatory truths that offer God's healing to the world, instead of still searching for or wondering if God still heals today!

❧Church Examination

Workbook Question: Does Your Church Have Symptoms of being sick?

For many, many Christians it may sound overly harsh and extreme to describe our churches as sickly, diseased and infertile with spiritually ineffectual children. Those who think so, however, may well be the very same Christians who are either sitting in a sick church, blind to the suffering and imminent death of their congregation or they are making excuses that it's all just the course of the world and the way things are, with nothing to be done. They may also be the same Christians who reject any "new" revelations of faith.

Week after week sick Christians sit in sick churches hoping for healing. In fact, there is the very real possibility that you may be reading this book now because you suspect your own church might be plagued with a spirit of infirmity.

And if your heart has ever ached for a change you thought the Church would provide; or hoped for an answer the Church should have had; or even longed for a miracle that should have been found in the midst of a House of the Presence of the Lord, then please be reassured – there is deliverance, healing and hope for the congregations of the world!

Whether you are a pastor, leader or member, you can diagnose the sicknesses plaguing your church in the same way a doctor will run tests to determine a health diagnosis over our physical bodies. But we know some individuals don't like to go to doctors! And, even when feeling badly they still won't go – as if not going and not knowing will stave off the inevitable.

By that same token, church members, leaders and pastors will attend a sick church, serve in a sick church or lead a sick church, knowing deep down that something isn't right, but without ever acknowledging what is wrong or making the attempt to diagnose what it is and determine how to cure it.

And yet, when a person does see a doctor and is diagnosed with an illness – and even if that person is a Christian – the process of cure and recovery will begin. Whether the next course of action is treatment through medicine and following the doctor's orders; treatment through prayer, faith and the laying on of hands or some combinations of both, the individual will readily do far more for their own natural bodies than a Believer (whether member, leader or pastor) will attempt to do for a Church that is suffering under sickness as well.

In centuries past the church was the place where an individual went for answers, for hope, for sanctuary and peace. Now the church is mistrusted, despised, disregarded, belittled and rejected. Most of which the church has brought on herself through abuse (both physical and financial); the mishandling of her members; lies; erroneous teachings and rampant sin that has caused even its pastors to succumb. Generally speaking, the Church is too sick to offer healing to anyone – like a doctor who smokes but tells you to quit.

However, so long as Jesus reigns – resurrected and alive, seated at the right hand of the Father, He will always be the Healer. We read the scriptures written thousands of years ago and we can receive Jesus as a healer, and with some prodding and instruction might also be able to accept that if Jesus is the same yesterday, today and forever (Hebrews 13:8), then He will be (and is) the Healer who lives within us. And so long as the Comforter, the Spirit of the Living Lord lives within the hearts and lives of His people, there is hope and healing still available to the Church and her Body.

Say that again!

So long as the Comforter, the Spirit of the Living Lord lives within the hearts and lives of His people, there is hope and healing still available to the Church and her Body.

God is not dead and neither is the promise of healing in His Word. Neither are His promises of healing for you and for the church you belong to, serve in or lead. God wants your natural body healed. Psalm 107:20 says God sent His Word for Healing. Well, Jesus is the Word and He wants His Church (His Bride) to be healed as well. Our Jesus is the Great Physician and only He has the medicine, the cure and the preventative measures necessary to heal the whole church – body and soul. And Jesus still desires to offer these to the world today, but He can only do so through a healed and whole church!

The appointment has been scheduled and it's time for a complete check-up and diagnosis for your body; the church body and the body of Christ.

It is time for God's truths for healing to be resurrected. And it is long past due for the Believer to actually believe in the truths and power that have been given to us through Jesus Christ! We can take matters into our own hands but only through Jesus and the Keys of the Kingdom that He has given to us - to lay hands on the sick[8] - even if that sickness is in our own natural bodies. Then, as we freely receive that healing and divine health through Jesus and the Word of Truth, we can then be free to bring healing to the whole body of the Church of Jesus Christ and into the world as well.

Chapter Summary

- The Church has life and is meant to live abundantly as the Bride of Christ – healthy and free of spot or wrinkle.

- The Church is meant to mature, from revelation to revelation, through faith in each new truth to the body.

- Much of the Church is now "normalized" – looking just like the world and suffering from the same problems.

- Pastors, leaders and members need to examine their churches to identify sickness and make a plan to heal.

DETERMINATION: Jesus is the Healer, yesterday, today and forever and He wants you and your church healed, well and whole.

Church Work Book

CHAPTER 1; LESSON 1

Each question has several multiple-choice statements. Rate each statement with an answer from 1-5. "1" = not at all; "5" = frequently. Add your answers and find the results on page 138.

1. **Is your church living or dying?**
   a. My church receives regular visitors
   b. My church regularly performs baptisms
   c. Members join my church and stay
   d. My church has a large youth ministry

2. **Is your church maturing?**
   a. Weekly messages are fresh and exciting
   b. Members give praise reports about change
   c. My church is a prosperous, giving church
   d. My church does work in the community

3. **Is your church "normal?"**
   a. Problems get solved with Biblical answers
   b. Our teens and young adults are happy kids
   c. We have a multi-generational church
   d. Our couples have strong, happy marriages

4. **Does your church have symptoms of being sick?**
   a. My church teaches healing for today
   b. Our members are fairly healthy
   c. We have an effective prayer department
   d. We have many miracle testimonies

Note: Each section has a possible rating ratio of 4-20 pts
Each chapter lesson has a possible rating ratio of 16-80 pts

2
℘*Wholeness*

✍*Church Math*

Workbook Question: What does 1+1+1 equal?

We know that our heavenly Father is a Triune God –
three in One – God the Father, God the Son and God the Holy
Spirit. And even though these three entities of God are each
individual with individual purposes and personalities – they are
still One and inexplicably linked as one – neither One is separate
from the other in their deity.[9] And like our Heavenly Father, we
– mankind – who were created in His image and in His likeness
were also created three in one – body, soul and spirit.[10]

Understanding the relationship between body, soul and
spirit was one of the greatest revelations I've received as a
Christian and it is vital to the understanding of the divine health
that God has provided for our physical bodies.

Before coming to salvation, our spirits were dead, killed
by the disease of sin and death running through our veins
through the blood of the first Adam by his disobedience to God.

And because of his transgression in the Garden, (as a result of Eve being deceived by the serpent), all of mankind is forever born into this iniquity that lives life by way of body and soul. We interact with the world through the five senses of our bodies and the information is stored in our souls – which is our mind, will, intellect, emotion, experiences and memories that ultimately make up our personalities.

By the time we do come to the saving knowledge of Jesus Christ, our souls are in charge. We make decisions according to our emotions and the resulting experiences cause us to react with more emotions! All the while, each negative emotion floods our bodies with hormones and chemicals causing imbalances and toxins that are further inflamed and aggravated by the thoughts, doubts and fears instigated by the enemy through the world and the various ways in which we interact with it through our five senses!

It's a vicious cycle that quickly becomes so normal that the opposing truths of the Word of God become foreign and nearly impossible to understand, accept or even follow.

Then, when we are reborn and our spirits are quickened unto new life, our "spirit man" (as described in 1 Corinthians 2:11 and 1 Corinthians 15:39-45), then battles the emotional distresses of our soul and the physical realities of bodies in order to bring divine unity and healing between these three entities – just as our Heavenly Father originally intended!

Like our Heavenly Father who is three in One – Father, Spirit and Son – our three entities of self are inexplicably linked, one to the other, not separate but each with a separate purpose within us. But unlike our Father in Heaven, as Christians our three entities of Being are often in total conflict with one another. So too are the individual Christians who make up the church; the local church body and the whole church body of those who are Believers in Jesus. These three also are inexplicably linked – three entities of one, separate but connected one to another and often in conflict with each other.

CHURCH NOTE:

YOU: *Are "The Church"*
YOUR CHURCH: *Is "The Church"*
ALL CHRISTIAN CHURCHES: *Are "The Church"*
*The Church isn't a place to go or a thing to have, but a thing to **be**.*

Christian basics often teach the Trinity. This truth is fundamental to our faith. We believe in Father, Son and Holy Spirit. And more advanced Christian teachings also describe the three in one entity of mankind just as Genesis 1:26 says - that we were created in the image and likeness of God. These are concepts the Believer can come to terms with, receive revelation from and adopt as a frame of reference for understanding God and ourselves in relation to our Christianity.

But when it comes to reconciling Christian principles against the average Christian's reality – our understanding of a Triune God and our own physical nature consisting of body, spirit and soul – do little to help us when we're in need of healing, when family members are on drugs, when loved ones die or houses go into foreclosure. And worse, the knowledge of a Heavenly Father, our Savior Jesus and the indwelling Comforter do little to soothe the wounds of a human body or soul that is hurt, damaged or abused by the very church meant to offer a solution and be a sanctuary to the ills of the world. What then will save us from the ills of the church?

❧Church Lessons

Workbook Question: What does your church believe?

Unfortunately, there does not seem to be a teaching on the fact that God is Father, Son and Spirit that will offer relief to the body wracked by sickness, or the Church who is suffering under sin. Neither does there seem to be a teaching on man being three in one that will offer the some solutions as well. But that doesn't mean these lessons aren't there to be found in God's Word – 3 John 1:2 gives us a clue that they are:

> *"Beloved, I wish above all things that you may prosper and be in health, even as your soul prospers."*

It is God's desire ***above all things*** is that we prosper in every aspect of our tangible, physical lives (outside of our own bodies); that we walk in perfect health within our bodies; and that our souls – our mind, will and emotions (our mental health) prosper as well. But this verse says that we will only prosper and be in health in direct proportion to how our souls prosper!

God wants His people to walk in three-fold prosperity: in the world, in our bodies and in our souls. But as Believers, our souls can only prosper by obeying (1 Peter 1:22) our spirit man through the Truth and Knowledge found in the Word of God – and John 1:1-3 & 14 say Jesus IS the Word of God!

Jesus is the Word of prosperity and healing for every area of our lives and through the examples of His ministry on earth we see specific healing answers for the questions of sickness and disease in the human body.

For those who believe that Jesus is still a healer today, these lessons are taught, expected and realized. And yet, far less realized is the truth that since Jesus [the Healer] established the Church and will return for the Church, there is much healing for the Church body in the scriptures as well.

Say that again!

Since Jesus, the Healer, established the Church and will return for the Church, there is healing for the Church body in the scriptures as well!

1 Corinthians 12:12-27 compares the human body to the body of Christ – which is, the Church of Christ. This analogy is far more literal than just a creative way to describe the functionality of the Church and how we as individuals must relate to one another with Christ as our Head. But instead, it is a truth that is reflected in our physical bodies and simultaneously within the church body as well.

If there is a need for healing in an individual Christian's body, then it is reflected in the body of Christ. And when you look at the physical state of many Believers, it is evident that collectively, individuals within the Church are more sick than healthy, and that our individual sicknesses, diseases and weaknesses are reflected collectively throughout the whole body of Christ – the Church. Therefore, the very same word that will bring healing to an individual will bring healing to the local Church. And likewise, any word that will heal the Church will be a healing truth necessary for the whole body of Christ.

Ecclesiastes 4:12 states that a three-fold cord is not easily broken. It is no wonder then that God has bound together many things in "threes." The Word, the Believer and the Church are no exception.

John 1:1-3 and verse 14 tell us without a doubt that Jesus is The Word. And again, 1 Corinthians 12 describes Him as the head of the Church – the same church that is compared to the human body. Therefore, it is quite reasonable to determine that if Jesus is the head of the Church, then the Word therefore is (or at least should be) the head of the Church – as well as the head of the individual Believer.

This is a concept easy enough to understand – and is also one that is taught in our Christian churches throughout the world. Jesus is the head of the Church, and many church denominations will acknowledge Jesus as "the Head of my life" before making a congregational announcement or corporate prayer. Therefore, by following any path of logic, it would stand to reason that the Word must be central to the Church as well as the life of the Christian. However, when we scrutinize any particular aspect of the local church or the Christian lives of its members, the application of the Word being the head of the Church and the Christian seem to become a bit muddied.

Church Grammar

Workbook Question: Does your Church need the Word?

No one denies that in His ministry upon earth, Jesus was a healer – right? And those who believe in healing for today will say that Jesus still is the Healer, correct?

Well, Hebrews 13:8 says Jesus is the same yesterday, today and forever. Therefore, if Jesus was the Healer yesterday, He is still the Healer today. And if Jesus was the Word yesterday, then the Word is definitely the Healer the Church needs for today.

Say that again!

If Jesus was the Healer yesterday, He still is
the Healer today. And If Jesus was the Word
yesterday then The Word is definitely
the Healer the Church needs for today!

The Word of God is Power. It is the power of God unto
salvation (Romans 1:16); it is the power that upholds all things
(Hebrews 1:3); and it is a power that is sharper than any two-
edged sword, piercing even to the dividing asunder of soul and
spirit, and of the joints and marrow, and is a discerner of the
thoughts and intents of the heart (Hebrews 4:12) – that's
describing our soul, spirit and body.

And just like our Triune God: Father, Son and Spirit, and
just like our own triple nature: body, soul and spirit – The Word,
The Church and our Bodies are a trinity of truth reflected in and
throughout each other. Our body, connected to the local body,
connected to the whole body of Christ is a truth that is largely
unknown. And the Church's lack of understanding these truths
has led to the inherent sickness of the Church and the overall
demise of health within the church body.

You are the Church and the Church is the Body of Christ.
Therefore, whatever illness you can suffer in your body, causes
suffering throughout the individual church and within the whole
body of Christ as well. This suffering is reflected throughout the
entire church body collectively, causing sickness in each Church.

But this Church-wide sickness is not just physical. Every illness has a spiritual root that easily infects the local church. These spiritual symptoms then go unnoticed and quickly spread throughout the body of Christ like a Cancer that metastasizes everywhere, evading both detection and treatment, ultimately killing its host with great pain, speed and voracity.

Church Understanding

Workbook Question: Is your church the Church?

The word "church" is an English word that was used as a translation for the Greek word "Ecclesia" when Jesus first used it in Matthew 16:18. He told Peter, "upon this rock I will build my church; and the gates of hell shall not prevail against it."

And even though Jesus uses the word "it" – He does not mean "the church" as a building or organization. He means the collective, called together group of individuals who will believe in Peter's same God-given revelation of Him as the Son of God, the Christ.[11]

It is the revelation of Jesus that builds the Church. And, it is that same revelation of Jesus that empowers the Church so that anything the devil and his demons might launch at her from behind their protective gates of lies and deception simply will not prevail! The Church is meant to storm hell's gates in victory!

This is why so many individual Christians lose the battle against Cancer, Diabetes, Depression and so many, many other sicknesses, diseases, pains and illnesses. They just do not understand the victory Jesus has given us already as a part of our salvation and revelation of Him as our Savior!

Jesus came to save us, yes from sin and death, but also from the destructive works of the devil. (1 John 3:8) And when we as the Church come to a more complete understanding, revelation and acceptance of that salvation well will not only live from a place of victory, but we will experience victory in our bodies through healing as well.

This victory in the individual body cannot stay within the physical body, but will be reflected in church body as well. Because the amazing thing about a church body is that while in my physical body, my elbow cannot pray for my hurt heel and my back cannot not pray for my headache, the church body is not the same. And so church members who receive healing have to pray for one another – pray for their leaders, pray for others who are suffering and pray for the church collectively.

As individuals we have to have personal understanding that we are connected to our local Church – not as a member in an organization we attend, but as a member one to another of a body of Believers. You are the Church as an individual member. And you are connected to other individual members of the congregation where you have your membership and attend services. But you are connected to the whole church body also.

Your local church congregation – its organization, structure, denomination and membership are all connected to other churches and each individual church combined with all other churches make up the church body collectively, as a whole.

And as individuals, we have a collective responsibility to the Church – to be healed and to heal. If we walk in wholeness as individual Christians, our local churches will walk in wholeness. And as our local churches begin to walk in wholeness so will the whole body of Christ.

But it has to start with a whole understanding of a Triune God, who made us in His image and in His likeness – three in one – with the intent that we would be one in Him.[12] Then, in our oneness in Him, we would walk in unity.[13] And it is through this unity of wholeness, health and well-being that the world will see there is a living, loving God who might desire their healing and wholeness as well.

Chapter Summary

- God has made the Church three-in-one like our bodies

- The Church is fully interconnected to the Word of God

- The Church has victory against the gates of hell

- As the Church receives healing, she should freely give [14]

DETERMINATION: As the individual Believer is healed through the revelation of Jesus as Healer, the local church will be healed and so will the whole church body of Christ.

Church Work Book
CHAPTER 2; LESSON 2

Each question has several multiple-choice statements. Rate each statement with an answer from 1-5. "1" = not at all; "5" = frequently. Add your answers and find the results on page 139.

1. **What does 1+1+1 mean to your Church?**
   a. One God: Father, Son and Holy Ghost
   b. Three in one: body, soul and spirit
   c. Unity in The Church Universal
   d. One Lord, one faith, one baptism[15]

2. **What does your Church teach?**
   a. We believe that only Jesus is the Healer
   b. We believe Jesus still heals today
   c. We believe God won't use sickness to teach
   d. Believers are anointed to heal the sick

3. **Does your Church need the Word?**
   a. The Bible has basic instructions for life
   b. The Word is the foundation of Christianity
   c. The Word is true and not for interpretation
   d. The Word holds the power for all our needs

4. **Is your Church the Church?**
   e. My church is a sanctuary for the needy
   f. My church has resources for the homeless
   g. My church offers counsel for non-members
   h. Members are recognized in the community

Note: Each section has a possible rating ratio of 4-20 pts
Each chapter lesson has a possible rating ratio of 16-80 pts

3
Sickness

≈Church Enemies

Workbook Question: Is your Church prevailing?

In Matthew 16:18 Jesus tells Peter and the other disciples, "upon this rock I will build my church and the gates of hell shall not prevail against it." Jesus is the Rock of our salvation and He has always intended to build His Church upon the revelation of Himself as the Christ, the Son of the Living God. (Matthew 16:16)

The English word "Christ" is "Christos" in the Greek and it means "Anointed One." This is the same word in Greek as "Messiah" in the Hebrew. Jesus is and always will be our Anointed One. And everything we see He was anointed to do in the pages of the word of God, He is still anointed to do in the life of the Church. Well, we are the Church! And when we live our lives with the anointed power of Jesus abiding and residing within us, we are to live a life that the enemies of God and the gates of hell cannot prevail against!

Say that again!

When we live our lives with the anointed power of Jesus within us, we will live a life that the enemy and the gates of hell cannot prevail against!

However, over generations of misunderstanding these verses regarding the gates of hell, the church now lives as if we cannot prevail against the onslaught of attacks that continually come at us from the enemy, making sinners and Believers alike, tolerate a type of hell on Earth until Jesus raptures us away from this worldly torment!

In truth, Matthew 16:18 states, that hell and all its demons do not have the power to withstand the attack of the Church that is fortified by the revelatory truth of Jesus Christ! The Church that Jesus desired to build, upon the revelation of Him, is a Church that should be on the offensive and not on the defensive! We should be advancing un-hindered upon the gates of hell with the same supernatural power of Jesus Himself, so much that the enemy can't tell us apart,[16] and the barricades of lies that the devil and his demons have set up to protect themselves cannot stand against our onslaught of truth!

We know the Way; we have the Truth and we are alive in Christ! Not only that, we've been given power[17] and the very keys to the Kingdom of binding and loosing. We should prevail!

But think about it, only the devil benefits from the Church getting Matthew 16:18 wrong! And the only way the enemy will (and does) prevail against the Church, is to keep the Church deceived about the depth of her power against his attacks! But our power as a Church is revealed through Christ!

CHURCH NOTE:

John 14:12 says that we shall do the works of Jesus and greater shall we do also. Many leaders say that "greater work" is the work of salvation and winning souls. But even if that is true, the Church still has the miraculous works that Jesus did to do as well!

ᕽ Church Anointing

Workbook Question: Is your Church like Jesus?

Jesus was the very first "Itinerant Preacher." His ministry is described in scriptures as one in which He went about "teaching and preaching that the Kingdom of Heaven was at hand; healing the sick; raising the dead; cleansing the lepers and casting out demons."

But Jesus did not choose his profession as many ministers do in the world – Jesus was sent and anointed to do the works that He did. And while no one else could cleanse us of our sin, Jesus is the example of what the Church should do.

The ministry of Jesus on Earth through His anointing described in Luke 4:18-19 is also the description of the ministry of every Church, if Jesus is its Head. And the anointing power of the Holy Ghost then becomes the power the Church has as well when individual members of the Church walk in the anointing of Jesus in their lives.

> *Luke 4:18-19*
> *"The Spirit of the Lord is upon me, because he has anointed me to preach the gospel to the poor; he has sent me to heal the brokenhearted, to preach deliverance to the captives, and recovering of sight to the blind, to set at liberty them that are bruised, To preach the acceptable year of the Lord."*

If Jesus is anointed to heal, then the Church will be anointed to heal when individual Believers walk in their healing anointing. If Jesus is anointed to prosper, then the Church will prosper as individual members prosper. And if Jesus is anointed to raise the dead or cast out lepers, the Church will be as well, but only as individual members of the church realize and walk in the anointing power of Jesus in their own lives through the baptism of the Holy Ghost.

But the enemy works hard to keep the Church and her leaders deceived, lied to, and confused about these logical but very supernatural truths that still pertain to the Church today!

ᔕ Church Deception

Workbook Question: Does your church believe the Truth?

When satan first showed up in the Garden of Eden to have a conversation with one of God's newly created beings, his first and most effective act of jealousy towards humankind was to cause Eve to be confused about what God had told them.

Genesis 3:2-3 *"And he said unto the woman, Yea, has God said, you shall not eat of every tree of the garden? And the woman said unto the serpent, We may eat of the fruit of the trees of the garden: But of the fruit of the tree which is in the midst of the garden, God has said, you shall not eat of it, neither shall you touch it, lest you die."*

Now, God never told Adam and Eve not to touch the tree. And there are a lot of things Christians (Pastors and Leaders too) believe about healing that God never said. God never said He would teach His people a lesson, or get their attention through sickness. Jesus never said He would pick and choose who to heal, if they were worthy. And honestly, God also never told us to just pray and hope for healing and leave the results (whether or not He will heal or not) up to Him.

It might seem like a minor thing that Eve told the serpent that God said "don't touch the tree." And you may not see what difference there is in getting sick so that God can teach you something, and God teaching you something through your sickness either – but they are entirely different situations.

Eve believed she would die if she touched the tree. But when she didn't fall over dead after plucking the fruit off of the tree, it then added fuel for her to believe satan's next lie:

Genesis 3:4 *"And the serpent said unto the woman, You shall not surely die:"*

Now that she'd touched the tree and grabbed the fruit and didn't die the way she thought God said she would, it was easier for her to believe that she wouldn't die from eating the fruit either.

This second tactic of deceit from the enemy remains the same today. First he confuses us about what the word of God says, then, through our confusion, and our natural experiences, he convinces us that God's word is wrong, isn't true or doesn't apply to us.

Sound familiar? Far too many Christians, Pastors and Leaders are convinced that God doesn't heal today; or that testimonies of divine healing just aren't true; or that God uses doctors to heal today because of the advancements of modern medicine that didn't exist before; or that maybe because of the sin in our lives (or lack of faith) we simply don't deserve or can't receive God's supernatural, miraculous healing in our bodies.

And even though we're talking about healing, the truth is these same lies of the enemy work against Believers in the areas of prosperity, deliverance, righteousness, faith, provision, purpose, power and so much more as well!

Finally, satan's last ploy of deception against God's children is exampled through Genesis 3:5. After telling Eve she surely would not die, he then put the final nail in their coffin of spiritual death by saying,

"...God does know that in the day you eat thereof, then your eyes shall be opened, and you shall be as gods, knowing good and evil."

Essentially satan is telling Eve (and Adam who was there with her[18]), that not only is God a liar, but He is withholding something good from them, something they want and something that will make them better!

Healing is **good**! And yes, even if we have a headache or the common cold, we will take medicine because even if we somehow believe God gets Glory from our illnesses and disease – we still **want** to be healed! And even as infants we inherently know, healing is **better** than being sick, miserable or in pain!

And yet, satan and satan alone has the Church of God believing that our good, good God withholds from his people the very healing we know is good; the healing we want and the healing we know will make us better!

But just like satan's lie to Adam and Eve – he had them convinced that God was withholding from them the very thing that God had already given them – and it was the very thing God had not just given to them, but worked into their DNA. Adam and Eve were already "like God" and so are we today! Mankind is still created in the image and likeness of God!

By that same reasoning, Healing is still for God's people today as well. Healing is ours – it's "the Children's Bread"[19] – given to us by God and worked into our DNA as Believers so that not only can we be healed, but we can lay hands on the sick and bring healing and recovery to others as well! [20] If we doubt that we can be healed, or doubt that healing is today, then we should doubt the doubt because only the enemy is behind it!

When Peter was teaching the Jews about eating meat in Romans 14, he commended them to reason by way of faith and not to be in doubt:

> Romans 14:23
> "And he that doubts is damned if he eat, because he eats not of faith: for whatsoever is not of faith is sin.

Eating wasn't the problem – doubting was. And doubt is not of faith, therefore doubt is a sin. And again, it is an effective ploy of the devil if he can get you to doubt your healing because he knows like James 1:5 says, if you waver in your faith you will not receive anything

It is time for the Church to stop believing the lies of the devil that say we cannot receive immediate, supernatural, divine and miraculous healing or have our elders anoint the sick with oil, [21] and pray for their recovery!

Yes, God heals through medicine and good doctors. But many doctors and nurses are members of sick Churches too!

∽Church Experience

Workbook Question: Is your church sick or ill?

And so now, we see a Church that is so complicit with the lies of the devil, that pastors, leaders and members will (centuries after the power and success of the early church), teach, defend and protect those lies of the devil and then hold up examples and experiences of their own lives to justify and perpetuate that which the enemy wants us all to believe.

But the truth of the matter is, we cannot and should not let the past experiences of our leaders, our friends, families or even our own bodies cloud, taint and distort the truth of the word of God. Scripture says, "Let God be true and every man a liar," and that has to be our fundamental truth even when we lie to ourselves. The world may state the facts about Flu season; our doctors may state the facts regarding our examination results; and pastors may state the facts regarding who died of what disease, regardless of their prayers. But the truth must always remain greater than the facts of our experiences. Jesus our healer is the same yesterday, today and forever and above all it is His desire that His Bride, the Church prospers and is in health even as our soul prospers! [22]

Say that again!

> **Jesus, our Healer, above all things, desires that His Bride, the Church might prosper and be in health, even as our souls prosper!**

Only the enemy wants the Church to be sick and works to keep her sick. And when Believers are sick and do not receive the healing Jesus died to give us, three things happen:

1. Individuals become offended by the word of healing in the scriptures and, like Jesus' own people in His own home town (which we are), we let our own disposition hinder our healing.

2. The sickness, disease or depression in our bodies make us too weak physically and emotionally to pursue our God-given purposes in power and in truth, and keep our time too consumed to serve our individual churches to effectively build the Kingdom of God. We become poor examples to the rest of the world as to why they would ever want to consider Jesus to save them from that which we are not saved from either.

3. And finally, when individuals can't serve or build their churches, and local churches have bad reputations for being "just like the world" then the whole church body is powerless to prevail against whatever "hell" the enemy and his demons heap upon the world! Thereby they remain in control and power as the rulers and princes of the kingdoms of the Earth!

Satan is a liar and there is no truth in him. [23] He has been The Deceiver since his debut in the Garden of Eden and he has not changed his tactics, wiles or mode of operation ever since. I guess he figures, if it ain't broke, don't fix it! But this is why Ephesians 6:11 says we must put on the "Whole Armor of God" that we might stand against the wiles of the devil.

Unfortunately, for far too long, Christians have not recognized (nor have they been taught) that sickness, disease, depression and all other maladies of the world are the "wiles of the devil" and they still blame God or give the credit to God Himself for the deficiencies in their bodies and minds (and money) and that of their family, friends, and congregations too!

- YOU are The Church – individual sickness in your body affects you as an individual Christian and church member.
- YOUR church is The Church – the sicknesses in the bodies of each member in your church affect that local church body.
- EVERY church is The Church – when whole churches are sick the whole body of Christ is sick, weak and ineffective.

CHURCH NOTE:

What the Pastor experiences; the members will experience.
What the member experiences; the whole Church experiences.
What the Church experiences; the whole body of Christ does too.
But when the Pastor teaches Truth and lives that which they teach, the whole Church body will experience the Truth of God!

It is an effective cycle of deceit that begins in the private life of each individual Christian (pastors and leaders included); it then bleeds unnoticed and unresolved into their local church; until finally it festers into an open, nasty and visibly ugly effect upon the whole church body! Unfortunately for us, we aren't able to sit in our yards by our fruit trees, bibles in our laps, checking the branches and limbs to see if the devil shows up so that we can catch him in his lies!

Today, the enemy's deception is far sneakier, covert and insidious. His lies show up in the most reasonable, legitimate, inconspicuous and commonly acceptable places, handed to us by the most respected, trusted and believable people. Friends, family, educators, political leaders, strangers in the store, Pastors, Christians, community leaders, and even our own children can be used by the enemy to convince us of his untruths. And, his most effective weapons against us are the very avenues we use to escape the trials, difficulties and hardships of this world: media, books, the internet, songs, movies, social media, TV and sermons from the pulpit!

So, let's analyze how the devil works his lies against us through the disease of diabetes. Pastors on Sunday erroneously preach that diabetes is a "Generational Sin." Then health commercials on TV and very many doctors will tell you that diabetes has a high rate of genetic disposition in certain families. You hear all of this and think, "Yeah, there are several people in my family with diabetes. I wonder if I'm at risk too?"

Then, you immediately call up your family members for details about their symptoms, and instantly you begin to determine whether or not you have symptoms as well. Next thing you know, you're craving donuts or feeling light-headed and convinced you have diabetes.

Then, unfortunately, after worrying for several weeks and counting up various symptoms, you finally decide to make an appointment and the doctor does indeed confirm that you do have "signs of diabetes in its early stages."

In this scenario, the enemy has easily and effectively hindered you from effectively walking in the Christian power and truth God has given you – the power and truth that has not been taught by your local church. Now you are concerned and anxious, instead of first praying for your family members that do have diabetes, and then praying for yourself and speaking against your own body succumbing to any of the symptoms.

This is the initial attack in which the enemy separates you from an active and effectual prayer life concerning your body and causes your own body to begin manifesting all the symptoms you've been dwelling on. (Proverbs 23:7a)

Then, when you have seen the doctor or had an annual exam in which you're told you have the early signs of diabetes, this is the second area that the enemy will use to hinder you from walking in an active and effectual prayer life. Instead of praying against the diabetes now, you listen to the doctor who tells you that diabetes in its early stages can be managed well with diet and exercise. You begin to accept his findings and think about change, but worry has always made you eat all the comfort foods you love, and your worry brings on a mild stage of depression that keeps you from being motivated to exercise.

The enemy is in. He's gained a foothold into your health and quickly builds up a stronghold in your mind regarding the diabetes as it progresses and gains control over your life.

The first aspect of this scenario is representative of your own individual health and how it affects you as a Christian. Once you, as an individual receive the doctor's diagnosis, you as a person – a whole being – then "have diabetes." Your conversation changes and you will begin to claim your own ailment. The diabetes is no longer merely a possibility but now officially affects your whole body. This represents how your own individual sickness affects your own individual church.

Then, as that diabetes gets progressively worse and various other members of your body begin to be affected – such as your eyesight, or nerve damage in your feet – this then is representative of how one church's sickness can begin to affect other churches as well. It could be churches within the same denomination, fellowship or church structure. Or it could be neighboring churches in the same community. The layers really are complex and happen very nearly simultaneously.

Each member's individual sicknesses then affect the health of the whole local church and the body of Christ as well.

1 Corinthians 12:12 – "For as the body is one, and hath many members, and all the members of that one body, being many, are one body: so also is Christ."

What one member of the body experiences, the other members do as well. Your pinky toe may be an insignificant member of your body. But if you stub it, your whole body will react! Your ears will ring, your head might pound, your eyes will squint shut, your heart will pound, your leg picks up your foot, the other leg hops and your hands might ball into fists from the pain. What one member experiences, the others will too. And so it is spiritually in the body of Christ as well.

- Your body gets sick and affects the other members of your own individual body.
- Your body gets sick spiritually and affects the other members of your church spiritually
- Your local church body gets sick and affects the health of other churches as well.

And unfortunately – especially when using diabetes as an example – our individual health, local church health and the health of the Church collectively does not just stop at poor health, but when blindness sets in, or limbs are amputated it is representative of individuals within the church body (including pastors) who fall back into sin (through blindness by false teaching) or who give up and abandon the church all together (amputating themselves from their faith) because their experiences do not match the truths of the word of God.

Ultimately, the whole body can shut down and dialysis would be inevitable. Toxins could build up within the blood stream and the individual is in danger of dying. And, as individuals are at risk of dying so are whole churches. More and more we see Pastors having to work full time jobs to sustain the church financially until churches close their doors either due to financial issues, low membership or burn out. Diabetes causes death within the body and functions begin to shut down or die and must be removed. The weaker the body, the more imminent death will become.

So it is with the local church. Christians have been saved by the shed blood of Jesus Christ. But the toxins of untruths are being built up in our Spiritual blood stream and it is slowly, effectively killing off Christians and causing churches local churches to close their doors and die. Not only that, but the respect and effectiveness of the Church in the world are weak and ineffectual as well.

Looking at the world today, we cannot let the enemy prevail against the very church that is meant to prevail against him! His work in the Earth is rampant – not just in the sickness and disease he inflicts upon mankind. Depression, suicide, mental health issues and addictions are all a result of his work. Poverty, lack, famine and filthy water in under-developed nations – that's the enemy's handy work too. Crime, hatred, racism, terrorism and war – the enemy uses men to cause it all.

Only the Church is meant to have the answers to the ills of the world. But so long as the enemy can keep the church sick and ignorant he will prevail. So long as a religious spirit permeates the church, keeping her from teaching, believing and walking in health, the enemy will continue to reign in the Earth. And so long as individual Believers do not believe they can be healed or be instrumental in the healing of others, the whole church body will remain powerless to prevail against the gates of hell.

Clearly healing is needed not just in the lives of individuals, but in the local churches; the whole church body and the world! Healing was the greatest evangelistic tool that Jesus used and it should be that of the churches as well! You are the Church - you can receive your own individual healing and do your part to bring healing to the world!

Chapter Summary

- The Church is meant to prevail against the gates of hell.

- The Church should walk in the same anointing as Jesus.

- The enemy keeps the Church deceived about healing.

- Personal experience shouldn't keep us from the Truth!

DETERMINATION: Individual Believers must believe the truth about healing while recognizing that sickness comes from the enemy and that his lies come from many different avenues.

Church Work Book
CHAPTER 3; LESSON 3

Each question has several multiple-choice statements. Rate each statement with an answer from 1-5. "1" = not at all; "5" = frequently. Add your answers and find the results on page 140.

1. **Is your Church prevailing?**
    a.   We see sickness as the wiles of the devil
    b.   We have an effective deliverance ministry
    c.   We hear testimonies of healing frequently
    d.   We have a Spiritually gifted Evangelist team

2. **Is your Church like Jesus?**
    a.   We preach and teach the Kingdom of God
    b.   We serve our community of neighbors
    c.   We walk in the fullness of Spiritual Gifts
    d.   We see signs, wonders and miracles[24]

3. **Does your Church believe the Truth?**
    a.   We believe by His strips we are healed
    b.   We believe our faith will make us whole
    c.   We believe healing is part of our atonement
    d.   We believe what we receive we freely give

4. **Is your Church getting sick?**
    a.   We have lots of healthy senior members
    b.   We have few cases of disease in the Church
    c.   Our church members are rarely absent
    d.   Our members are fit, healthy and happy

Note: Each section has a possible rating ratio of 4-20 pts
Each chapter lesson has a possible rating ratio of 16-80 pts

4
Health

Church Ministry

Workbook Question: Does your Church administer the Word?

We know that when we look at Jesus in the scriptures, we see His ministry as proof of healing in the Word of God. And if we are to apply His healing truths to us as Believers today, we usually do so through Isaiah 53:5 "But he was wounded for our transgressions, he was bruised for our iniquities: the chastisement of our peace was upon him; and with his stripes we are healed." Or more especially through its New Testament counterpart in 1 Peter 2:24 – "Who his own self bare our sins in his own body on the tree, that we, being dead to sins, should live unto righteousness: by whose stripes ye were healed."

In many cases, "by His stripes we are healed" is the only verse of healing Christians know – and actually it is a slight but significant mix of both the Old and New Testament verses. "By" comes from the NT quote and "are" comes from the Old.

Isaiah is prophesying an event that, at the time, had not happened. And yet, he speaks in the present-tense saying, "with His stripes we *are* healed." Not too many will notice, let alone question Isaiah's choice of wording – not even when comparing it to the version Peter quotes. But not only are both accurate to the time in which they were spoken, but both become powerfully accurate to the New Testament Christian who recognizes the difference.

Isaiah was saying prophetically that there is a definite truth and result of the wounds Christ would suffer at His crucifixion. And that *with* every lashing man(kind) is and are to be healed. Then Peter refers to the actual crucifixion which, at the time of His speaking has already past and he declares that *by* every lash to our Savior's body, man(kind) *was* healed.

So, now – 2000+ years later – every Christian who comes to Salvation can still know that even though it was so many centuries ago, we all *were* healed when Jesus went to the cross. Our healing was purchased *with* the torture He received and we now we receive that blood bought healing *by* or because of each lash given from that "Cat of Nine Tails" whip.

Healing has already happened for the Believer in Christ and Pastors need to believe it in order to teach it in Truth to their members. Individuals then need to believe it so they can receive that healing provision in their bodies and walk in divine health. And individual Church bodies need to believe it so they can walk in a successful healing ministry just like Jesus did.

Scripture tells us we can lay hands on the sick and they shall recover (Mark 16:18); or that we can go to the elders to have them anoint us with oil, pray and we shall be raised up (James 5:14-15). In searching the Word of God (both through the works of Jesus and the declarations of His healing provision for us), we can find not only hope for our individual healing, but also instructions for operating healing ministries in our churches.

However, few churches facilitate such a healing ministry today. You can walk in any given church, in nearly every denomination and it will be a rare thing to find "Healing & Deliverance" as a normal part of the service, right along with "Praise & Worship" or "Tithes & Offering." And even in a church that might pray and ask for healing or possibly even lay hands on the sick and command healing, it will still be a unique find to see the Mothers Board, Sr. Deacons; Chief Stewards and other Elders of the congregation participating in their divinely assigned offices of "Church Healers."

Because pastors, leaders and church denominations miss, overlook or reject that the Word of God gives us instruction, permission and the word of power for the demonstration of its power to walk in boldness for healing, it is even more understandable that the church also misses out on (or at least does not "connect the dots" for) solutions, answers and healing scriptures for specific maladies, diseases and physical issues as well. And as a result, they suffer in silence.

❧Church Diagnosis

Workbook Question: Is your Church secretly suffering?

1 Corinthians 5:7 is a very unique and specific verse that is a perfect example of a "hidden health truth" in the Word of God. The scripture above is directed towards intimate relations between husbands and wives, and it says:

*"Defraud ye not one the other, except it be with consent for a time, that you may give yourselves to fasting and prayer; and come together again, that Satan **tempt** you not for your **incontinency**."* (bold added for teaching application)

In the Strong's Concordance (#192) "Incontinency" is defined as: want of self-control; incontinence or intemperance. We are taught that this refers to sexual immorality. And, yet in one other place in the bible, incontinence is defined as "excess."

However, in today's vernacular "incontinence" has an entirely different definition. It is one that actually can apply when we utilize the understanding of the definition of the word as "excess" and also when we look at the complete definition of the word "tempt" – which includes the idea of "forcing evil" upon a person.

So then, when we look at this verse from a new perspective we can see a warning from God that says husbands and wives should not withhold or refrain from sexual intercourse because the enemy can use that as an opportunity to cause you to be (or force your body to be) incontinent –

which is not having control (self-control) over one's own bladder or releasing an excess of urine without the appropriate bodily stimulation generally associated with urination.

Husbands love your wives! Wives, respect your husbands! Married couples have a choice to come together regularly in intimate, healthy sexual relationship, or, they can both invest in "adult underwear" as a normal part of growing older and "maturing" in their marriage. In truth, there are many men and women who suffer in silence and embarrassment from incontinence. This is how the enemy affects our physical bodies and deceives us into thinking it's just a normal part of aging.

But if a pastor could know who was suffering from incontinence in a congregation, they might see younger widows and widowers in the church, or the same ratio of divorces in their church as in the world. Or perhaps, after some careful questioning and counseling, pastors might also find unhappy, loveless, abusive or habitually unfaithful marriages amongst their "older" Christian generation. And, in making even just this one often missed discovery, pastors could potentially affect much healing in the secret lives of their congregations!

We know 1 Corinthians 5:7 is saying not to withhold sexual intimacy from one another in a marital relationship. And, if we are taught these verses, we are given the understanding that by defrauding one another from sex within marriage, the enemy can use this as an open opportunity to tempt you or your spouse into extracurricular marital relations – or adultery.

CHURCH NOTE:

Pastors often turn a blind eye to the sickness and suffering of their members out of a sense of protecting their privacy. But often times, Holy Spirit has revealed certain truths through the Gift of Discerning of Spirits, in order for the Pastor to be of help!

But now we can see that what might have only been a private problem from one individual to the next now looks like a church-wide issue affecting marriages. And since we know that marriage is God's example of the Lord's relationship with the Church, if we were to back up and look at marriages in the local church, we would clearly see the enemy's influence upon them. And when we take a step back even further and look at the whole church body we can even more clearly see evidence of incontinence in the Body of Christ by both of its definitions.

Christians are tempted by the enemy to commit spiritual adultery, fornicating with every worldly doctrine and belief, trying to fake their Christian commitment to Christ while having their worldly cake and eating it too. Denominations "tweak" their doctrinal truths to comfort, explain or accept the hard-to-understand situations of their members, and Christians are living in the same worldly excesses as their neighbors, with little self-control; without proper (or natural) stimulation; or the ability to manage the waste in their lives!

Say that again!

Christians are living in the same excesses as the world, with little self-control or the ability to properly manage the waste in their lives!

My prayer for you, whether pastor, leader or church member is as Elisha prayed for the eyes of his young servant, that your eyes will be opened as his were opened to see the protection of the Lord surrounding them in the midst of their enemy all around.[25]   The enemy has encircled the church but it is only through a refreshed spiritual perspective of the word of God, that the Church will prevail against satan and be healed!

Church Deliverance

Workbook Question: Can your Church be healed?

Looking at scripture from this "refreshed" perspective does not at all change the way in which we originally view the Word of God, or its truth. Nor does it affect an inaccurate meaning when we look at the verses with a more in-depth understanding of the original language or the way in which we use (or define) words today. These are the layers of truth and life and power that exist in the verses of God's word!

Ephesians 6:13-18 says, "*Wherefore take unto you the whole armour of God, that you may be able to withstand in the evil day, and having done all, to stand. Stand therefore, having your **loins** girt about with truth, and having on the **breastplate** of righteousness; And your **feet** shod with the preparation of the gospel of peace; Above all, taking the **shield** of faith, wherewith you shall be able to quench all the fiery darts of the wicked. And take the **helmet** of salvation, and the **sword** of the Spirit, which is the word of God: Praying always with **all prayer** and supplication in the Spirit, and watching thereunto with all perseverance and supplication for all saints;"*

We know these verses well in regard to being dressed in the whole armor of God, but we do not ever really consider these verses in regards to healing in our physical bodies.

In fact, it is still rather rare for teaching on these verses to include prayer in the list of armor as well. However, prayer in the Spirit is without a doubt included in these seven items of protection and defense against the wiles of the enemy because it builds and edifies the Believer in body, soul and spirit.[26] And, when we apply the "whole armor of God" not just as an analogy for our well-dressed spirits, but also as the only clothing option for the entire body of Christ, we will see that these verses offer opportunities to not only diagnose symptoms of sickness, weakness or disease in the Church, but also provide a guideline for potential healing and deliverance for the whole church body as well.

Here are the categories as listed in the passage:

1. **Loins** ...girt about with **truth**

2. **Breastplate** ...of **righteousness**

3. **Feet** ...shod with the preparation of **the gospel of peace**

4. **Arm/Hand** (...to take) the shield of **faith**

5. **Head/Neck** (...covered by) the helmet of **salvation**

6. **Mouth/Teeth** (...to speak) **the Word** – sword of the Spirit

7. **Mind/Wholeness** ...praying with all **prayer** and supplication

These scriptures not only outline the area or region of the physical body that might be affected by the enemy; but they also reveal the location of the spiritual battle fields, as well as the solution for victory in the fight!

And, with carful application and belief in the Word of God, through the Spirit of Truth, we (as Christians) will see victory not only in our individual bodies, but also in our local churches and thereby throughout the whole body of Christ. But it will have to take the whole body of Christ coming together in the unity of faith and understanding of these truths for us to begin to see the effects of this change within the world.

It can be done however, and it starts with you as you are reading, learning and applying these truths. When you begin walking in divine healing you will provoke your fellow Christians to Christ's good works of healing in them.

✺Church Change

Workbook Question: Can your leaders make a difference?

Hebrews 10:24-25
"And let us consider one another to provoke unto love and to good works: Not forsaking the assembling of ourselves together, as the manner of some is; but exhorting one another: and so much the more, as you see the day approaching."

If you are a member, leader or pastor, you can affect change in your one church. Healing in the Word of God is a "good work." And as you begin to change the way you look at healing in the Word of God, you will begin to manifest change in your own body. Once you walk in change, you will begin to provoke a desire for change amongst the other members in your local church. Then, as your one church begins to walk in more and more healing, collectively they will provoke another Believer or leader that is a member of a different church in the same denomination or community to desire healing as well.

But again, it starts when one person sees the healing truths in the Word of God and begins to walk in what they believe.

Ephesians 6:13-18 offers us the most comprehensive source for change and healing offered in the scriptures. From head to heel these verses offer a starting place for us to apply

God's divine health to our whole bodies: individually, church-wide and towards the whole body of Christ.

When we analyze the verses in Ephesians, part by part, we will see God has made provision for our bodies from head to heel; top to bottom; and in all the areas where we might suffer. Ordinarily preachers and teachers expound upon 6 parts of the "Whole Armor of God" – however, "6" is the number biblically associated with man, not God. So, we will analyze seven parts of His Armor for us and how to get dressed in His protection.

Ephesians 6; Verse 14:

"Stand therefore, having your loins girt about with truth,"
- "**Loins girt** with **truth**"

Armor Area #1 - Loins:

"Loins" is most definitely a word we do not use today! So, let's appropriately define what this portion of the verse is talking about.

The region of your loins covers your pelvic area, which include your reproductive and digestive systems. This region can also refer to our core or center or gravity as well as portions of our lower back and hips.

- Reproductive systems generally suffer from:
  1. Infertility
  2. Impotence
  3. Tumors or Growths
  4. Pain due to deformity or irregularity (women)
  5. Sexually Transmitted Diseases
  6. Cancer

- Digestive systems generally suffer from:
    1. Irritable Bowell Syndrome
    2. Acid Reflux
    3. Diarrhea or Constipation
    4. Indigestion or Heart Burn
    5. Crohn's Disease
    6. Cancer

Armor Item #1 - Girt with Truth:
"Girt" or "to gird" means to bind, or be bound; supported; physically restrained, contained or upheld.

This is our means of battling an attack of the enemy against our loins – whether physically or spiritually.

But first, we must diagnose the issue by taking a closer look at the attack. If a person is struggling physically in the area of their loins – first determine the type of issue and what's really going on. For example, infertility is a result of barrenness, lack of productivity or life; being stalled, unfruitful or halted in creativity. Cancer is a mutation of the normal functionality of the cells, foundation or original activity or creation of those cells and thereby that body part of function.

So, then once the physical issue is identified, we can ask, where then is the person's life affected by the same issue or understanding of self? Perhaps satan has convinced the person who is suffering from infertility that they would never accomplish anything in life; never amount to anything good, could never do anything right or was worthless.

Now, apply this destructive thinking to a church body that has many individuals suffering from infertility. If each individual feels worthless; hopeless and incapable of doing anything productive in life, then those individuals do not feel they have a purpose or function that would add growth to their church or add life to the Kingdom of God.

Add these individuals to the ones that have a prostate cancer, because of a mutated idea of their original purpose, image or function in life and the Kingdom; and to the people who have acid reflux who are convinced everything they touch will backfire into a colossal failure, and the one or two who have Crohn's Disease as a result of a twisted self-image and feeling that they don't belong or that the world was better off without them (like a portion of their intestines that was better off cut out of their bodies) – these people are members of the body.

In a small local church there may only be one or two or a few suffering from each separate malady. But collectively they make for a church body being attacked by the enemy in their loins so that individual congregation is barren, constipated and on the verge of dying from spiritual cancer.

Add this one church to a denomination with the same types of issues throughout all their churches; or a community where the neighbors who attend different denominations are suffering from similar issues and you can now see how one person's private illness, sickness, pain or suffering then affects their church body and the that church body affects the whole body of Christ.

But according to Ephesians 6:14, if the church is going to put on the "Whole Armor" of healing for their spiritual loins, then we're going to do it by girding up, shoring up and supporting each individual with the truth of the Word of God.

Yes, lay hands on one another and tell the irritable bowels "peace, be still in the name of Jesus." And yes, we should have the elders of the church anoint the bodies riddled with cancer with oil and pray that the cancer die, be pulled up by the root and cast into the sea. But if pastors, leaders and members do not deal with the root of the issues in the soul – the mind, will, emotions – where the enemy has them deceived and lied to, then that individual runs the risk of not receiving their healing, having the sickness return or at the very least will still hinder the church body, locally and collectively, with the same spiritual symptoms of the physical issue they were healed of, because they were only healed and not made whole.

CHURCH NOTE:

- *At salvation our spirits are reborn complete, perfect and whole*
- *But our physical sicknesses all begin from within our soul*
- *We must treat spiritual healing like the common cold*
- *feed the spirit (the Word) and starve (the lies from) the soul*

So, with the understanding of how to apply the Whole Armor of God physically, emotionally and spiritually, let's look at an overview of the rest of our protection and our solutions:

Ephesians 6; Verse 14:

"Stand therefore, having your loins girt about with truth, and having on the breastplate of righteousness;"

- **"Breastplate** of **righteousness"**

Armor Area #2 - Breastplate:
"Breastplate" is also a word we definitely do not use today! So, again, let's specifically detail what this portion of the verse is referring to.

The breastplate was a covering over the shoulders and in front of the heart, ribs and down to stomach. The High Priest wore a decorative breastplate called an "Ephod" held by straps over the back. But a breastplate meant for battle generally covered the back as well, with closures at the sides under the arms.

- The chest and back areas generally suffer from:
  1. Heart Failure or Disease
  2. Clogged Arteries
  3. Palpitations or Murmurs
  4. Circulatory Issues
  5. Respiratory Issues
  6. Lung Disease/Lung Cancer
  7. Broken Ribs
  8. Back Spasms/Muscle Spasms
  9. Slipped or Ruptured Discs
  10. Curvature of the Spine

Armor Item #2 – Righteousness:
     The breastplate, of course, provided a measure of protection to the vital organs of the main portion of the body from the front and the back. The most primary of all the organs would be the heart. In the natural, heart disease is one of the primary factors of death, especially in the United States.

However, lung disease, lung cancer and back issues and muscle spasms (especially due to stress) all compete for high ranking on the list of everything people currently suffer from.

Proverbs 4:23
"Keep your heart with all diligence; for out of it are the issues of life."

Ordinarily we would separate this verse referring to our spirit or "spiritual hearts" from our physical heart, but there is a connection. Jesus tells us in Luke 4:18 that one of the reasons He came was to "heal the broken hearted." And so, while there are many issues of the heart that are physical, there are many that are emotional as well. All of which must be dealt with through the protection and understanding of our righteousness.

Whether we suffer from heart disease, ruptured discs or lung cancer, our physical issues are rooted and grounded in the heart. And even when our issues are lack of provision, lack of joy,[27] strife and frustration,[28] immaturity,[29] or legalism,[30] the root cause of our problems can be solved by our righteousness.

But in any of the areas in which we suffer in our bodies or in our lives, if we just focus on the physical by praying the prayer of faith, laying hands or anointing with oil for healing and do not deal with the root, we will either see illnesses healed but return worse or not healed at all.

When Jesus cursed the fig tree,[31] his disciples said,
"Look Master, the tree you cursed is withered from the roots."
And when Jesus gave instructions on faith he told us we could
speak to the Sycamine tree and tell it to be "plucked up by the
roots and cast into the sea," and it should (or would) obey us.[32]
Embedded in the surface truth of the "Whole Amor of God" are
the various types of spiritual weed killer necessary for killing the
very root of every disease, sickness, ailment and problem the
enemy has been inflicting upon and infecting the body of Christ
with since the Garden!

It is well past the time for pastors and leaders to not
simply be under-shepherds of their flocks, guiding them to a mix
of the food and water of the Word and their own experiences –
treating their members as if they are sheep with a buffet choice
of what type of grass they prefer the pastor to feed them.

Instead, not only should pastors cultivate the pure and
rightly divided seed of the Word of God for their flocks to eat,
but it is also time for us all to be the husbandmen of the
gardens of our hearts and use the Word of God to get down to
the roots and curse the source of all our issues as well!

Say that again!

It is time to be the husbandmen of our hearts
and use the Word of God to root out and curse
the source of all our issues and diseases!

Ephesians 6; Verse 15:

"And your feet shod with the preparation of the gospel of peace;"

- "**Feet** shod with the **preparation of the Gospel of peace**

Armor Area #3 – Feet:

To have your feet "shod" meant wearing a sandal that was built for protection. A portion went up the leg, possible to the knee and straps were crossed about it to secure it to the leg.

Therefore the feet and legs represent your stance or position in life; your foundation or belief system; as well as your walk of life; your Christian walk or the direction your life is going.

Feet can tend to suffer from:
1. Bone Spurs
2. Bunions
3. Fallen Arches
4. Plantar Fasciitis
5. Athletes Foot
6. Ingrown Toenails

These physical issues could be (emotionally) associated with:
1. An added, new, difficult or, painful life circumstance
2. A hard, obstruction or obstacle or new development
3. Betrayal, no support, feeling flat, lifeless or devastated
4. Extreme or deep-seeded pain, suffering or trauma
5. Being treated poorly, negatively or badly by others
6. Drastic self-image or abasement; treating yourself badly

Armor Item #3 – The Preparation of the Gospel of Peace:

Combining these possible issues to issues the legs might suffer from such as "Varicose Veins," would then reveal that the source of healing for these types of physical problems can only be found through the preparation of the Gospel of Peace.

What does that mean? Well, Jesus is the Prince of Peace,[33] and only He can give us a peace that surpasses understanding,[34] – not like the world can give.[35]

But when you find your life is suddenly and inexplicably struck by divorce, death, deep betrayal or trauma only the peace of Jesus can provide healing. And the more your life is prepared with Jesus, by Jesus and through Jesus, when times are good, happy, healthy and peaceful, the more you will be prepared to handle any curve ball the enemy throws from left field.

Unfortunately, when a life is not prepared, shored-up and "shod" with the preparation of the Gospel of peace, and terrible life circumstances altar the direction you're going, your walk of life or even your belief system, if those roots are left untended to, they may be left to fester and manifest into the very real, physical and painful issues suffered through our feet and legs.

Where do you and your church stand when it comes to healing and wholeness in the body of Christ? The answer to that is more obvious than we think, and the solution is in the Gospel!

CHURCH NOTE:

- *Our physical bodies give us clues to the source of our ailments*
- *Our churches are road maps to problems Christians are facing*
- *The Church Body is a billboard of weakness in the whole church*
- *The world is watching and attributing these signs to "religion"*

Ephesians 6; Verse 16:

"Above all, taking the shield of faith, wherewith ye shall be able to quench all the fiery darts of the wicked."

- "Shield of Faith, quenching fiery darts"

Armor Area #4 – (Shield Held by...) Hand/Arm:

First and foremost, a shield is held by the hand supported by the arm. And while this analogy for our physical bodies is accurate, it is even more effective to also include and understanding of the "shield" as understood from these verses.

The description of a shield used at this time was a "four-cornered" shield, large enough to "surround" a warrior's body. Faith is meant to surround us; protect us and defend off whatever the enemy attacks us with physically.

Armor Item #4 – Faith:

While we can, like the other "Armor Items," apply the shield of faith to our physical hands and/or arms and the ailments that might attack them, it is more accurate and physically beneficial to look at how the bible uses references to hands and arms to see the fullness of the healing that is afforded to us through our faith.

Generally, the arm was used in reference to one's strength; while the left hand usually relates to provision and the right hand was used in relation to righteousness. And because the power of our hands greatly rely on the strength of our arms; these three aspects of this verse then are interdependent upon the others.

Therefore, every physical weakness in our bodies, as well as every tangible weakness in our finances or in our sense of righteousness in Christ is a direct result of the fiery darts of the enemy, and they can only be healed through faith in God's word!

Ephesians 6; Verse 17:

"And take the helmet of salvation,"

- "Helmet of Salvation"

Armor Area #5 – (Helmet) Head/Neck :

Let's be honest: headaches are a commonly accepted function of the natural world in which we live and chronic Migraines are just as widespread.

Various forms of depression, from mildly depressed to severe mental disorders have also been a long since epidemic in society – so much so that suffering from neck and shoulder pain due to stress is almost expected.

It's easy to assume that the "Helmet of Salvation" would cover these areas of disorders and issues. However, what is not always considered as that these helmets may also have had a face plate with a welded in grate to protect the eyes as well.

Therefore, in the physical sense of our healing, the "Helmet of Salvation" also covers our eyes (both physical and spiritual vision); emotional states; peace of mind; ears and hearing (both physical and spiritual) as well as nose; throat, mouth and teeth.

Armor Item #5 – Salvation:

You may or may not be wondering then, how our Salvation would have any effect on our healing in any of these areas.

If you already understand the Greek definitions of the words "Sozo" (saved) and "Sotario" (salvation), then you are probably among the ones who are not necessarily wondering how our salvation provides healing.

In fact, through a combined definition of the two words, as well as a concise list of all the various definitions from several Strong's Concordance versions, we see that salvation provides more than just deliverance from sin and entry into heaven.

The full definition includes <u>all</u> of these aspects of being saved:
1. Protection
2. Healing
3. Deliverance
4. Eternal Salvation (saved from sin & eternal damnation)
5. Abundant Life (abundance; sufficiency and wealth)
6. Long Life (length of days; saved from physical death)
7. Wholeness or Shalom (well-being and peace of mind)

When you relate this exhaustive definition with the "helmet" of our salvation, then you must not forget that first and foremost, a helmet protects our head and our heads protect our brains and our brain is where we think; store memories; learn and control every other function of our bodies.

It is no wonder even science professionals believe that most diseases begin in the brain or that most doctors know that a person's mental state will greatly affect their healing and recovery. That's why we need the "Helmet of Salvation."

Our soul is defined as our mind; our will (or desire); our intellect (how we learn and what we have knowledge of), and our emotions. Only the full knowledge of our salvation in Jesus Christ and all that God offers to us through it can provide healing and wholeness in all areas of our lives.

Say that again!

Only the full knowledge of all that Jesus offers to us through our salvation can provide us with healing and wholeness in every area of our lives!

Ephesians 6; Verse 17:

"And the sword of the Spirit, which is the word of God:"

- "Sword of the Spirit, the Word of God"

Armor Item #6 – Sword of the Spirit:

Often times we might hear of the bible itself being referred to as a "sword" or a weapon, or that the written word of God is the "Sword of the Spirit. However, in this verse, the term "word" is "rhema" in the Greek, which is the spoken word of God.

And, the context of how Paul used this phrase "the sword of the Spirit," is closely linked to use of the phrase "two-edged sword" throughout the word of God. A "two-edged" sword is frequently used in scripture with the word "mouth" because the literal translation of two-edged sword is a two "mouthed" sword. It is the way in which the word of God is rightly divided.[36]

Armor Area #6 – (Spoken Word of God) Mouth/Teeth:

Therefore, the "rightly divided" word, which is the rhema word of God, is the kind of word in which we speak over ourselves.

This then, as well as "putting on the helmet of salvation," become the two most important factors of our healing and divine health.

1. What do you think about healing?
2. What do you believe about the word of God?
3. What do you feel about your current health concerns?
4. What does your mental "self-talk" sound like?
5. Do your church leaders speak healing over you?
6. Do you speak the promises of God over yourself?
7. Do you tell your body what to do and how to do it?[37]
8. Do you speak words of healing faith to others?

Ephesians 6; Verse 18:
"Praying always with all prayer and supplication in the Spirit, and watching thereunto with all perseverance and supplication for all saints;"
- "Praying with all prayer"

Armor Item #7 – All Prayer:
The Church does not pray. Collectively, or as individuals, the church does not maintain a lifestyle of 1 Thessalonians 5:17 – to "Pray without ceasing."

And before you defend yourself or your church, answer this: when was the last time your entire congregation prayed? Or when have 120 members of your church ever gotten together for a 50 day, 24 hour prayer vigil, remaining on one accord?

This was the state of the First Church of Jesus Christ at the time of His resurrection, just before Pentacost. It is an event that few churches are able to recreate and therefore, collectively, the Church as a whole does not pray – let alone, pray with all [the biblical types of] prayer; and supplication [for oneself]; in the spirit; with perseverance; and with supplications for all saints (or in other words: intercession for other Believers).

Armor Area #7 – Soul/Spirit:
One of the most significant areas of prayer that the church widely neglects (or is ignorant or even fearful of), is praying in the Spirit. It is an <u>ability</u> that is <u>available</u> to all[38] Believers, that is separate from the gift of "divers tongues"[39] which is a supernatural gift of the Spirit.[40]

Jude 1:20
"But you, beloved, building up yourselves on your most holy faith, praying in the Holy Ghost,"

Praying in the Spirit (or in the Holy Ghost), actually
builds you up in complete wholeness – spirit, soul and body.
1 Corinthians 4:14 says that when we speak in tongues we edify
ourselves (our whole selves), and "edify" means "to build up."

This building up is not just in our spirit, but it is *from* our
spirit, *through* our souls, *to* our physical bodies. You see, the
term "edify" was used in terms of a building. You edify, fortify
or build up the edifice on a building or physical structure. And
1 Corinthians 3:9 says that we are God's building!

So that even when leaders are speaking and teaching
divine healing in the Word of God; church membership can still
miss the manifestation of those teachings if praying in the Spirit
is not taught as well.

Praying in the Spirit works in conjunction with all the
ways in which we are healed or maintain our divine health. And
without it, the bodies of our congregations are easily left in
their dilapidated, deteriorating and decimated states of being,
as if we've been taught how to build a house and have been
given a hammer, a saw and wood, but no nails.

If you are able to rightly divide the word[41] for healing in
your body, then praying in the Spirit provides the nails that hold
the pieces of the word together in the structure of your life.

If you feel in your soul that your life is falling apart then
praying in the Spirit is the nail that holds it all together. So that
either way, praying in the Spirit builds our lives with complete
wholeness, especially when we know not what to pray for.[42]

Symptoms in an individual's body that go unnoticed or undiagnosed are symptoms that will still manifest within the congregation, either spiritually or emotionally. These become church-wide symptoms that while they may be undiagnosed or unrecognized, they most definitely do not go unnoticed!

Far too many older; traditional, struggling, sick or dying churches are generally filled with "Church Folk" as members. "Church Folk" are easily spotted because they tend to be the members who are critical, bitter, mean, selfish, stingy, cranky and disagreeable. They may be ungrateful, unwilling to grow or change and can spread their "religious spirit" to other members.

If pastors and leaders were to use Ephesians 6:13-18 as a guide or "decoder ring" for the emotional, financial and health issues in the church, most of what is infuriating or frustrating about "Church Folk," might just be clues as to how bring healing to their bodies, souls and lives, as well as the whole Church.

Chapter Summary

- Jesus' ministry in the Word should be an example to us.

- There are clues to our health "hidden" in the Word

- Scripture can be applied literally to our lives for healing

- All natural issues are connected to spiritual solutions

DETERMINATION: The Word of God has the power to determine physical and emotional symptoms in our bodies and churches, as well as offer spiritual solutions to every natural problem.

Church Work Book
CHAPTER 4; LESSON 4

Each question has several multiple-choice statements. Rate each statement with an answer from 1-5. "1" = not at all; "5" = frequently. Add your answers and find the results on page 141.

1. **Does your church administer the Word?**
    a. We recognize healing in the Word of God
    b. Our church believes we are already healed
    c. We see miracle healings in our church
    d. Our church has the healing ministry of Jesus

2. **Is your church secretly suffering?**
    a. We know all scripture is applicable for life
    b. We have the same issues as other churches
    c. Our leaders are full examples of the Word
    d. We know every issue has a spiritual source

3. **Can your church be healed?**
    a. We believe there is power in the Word
    b. We seek the word for answers to problems
    c. We believe God uses doctors to heal
    d. We speak directly to every health issue

4. **Can your church leaders make a difference?**
    a. We are a community beacon for healing
    b. We recognize prayer as an Armor of God
    c. Everything natural is connected spiritually
    d. Our leaders teach us to pray in the Spirit

Note: Each section has a possible rating ratio of 4-20 pts
Each chapter lesson has a possible rating ratio of 16-80 pts

5
Healing Your Body

❦Church Tools:

Workbook Question: Is your Church prepared to be healed?

There is no confusion as to the state of the world's health. Sure, healthcare has progressed and great advances in medicine and research have been made. And yet look at the statistics that still exist for diseases like Cancer, Diabetes and Heart Disease. More individuals are diagnosed annually with Lupus, Eczema or Fibromyalgia. Mutant strains of Flu and Ebola spread fear throughout the world just as quickly as the viruses themselves are spread. And for many, Hypertension, Arthritis and Osteoporosis are just the common side effects of aging.

Despite health trends in Organic foods, healthier diets and the promotion of a more active lifestyle, America remains overweight by majority and the reality show "My 600 lb. Life" would not suffer for participants if the show stayed on air for years to come.

America is dying and the slow death is starting at an earlier age as year after year more and more children are stricken with "Childhood Diabetes" and strains of Cancer thought only to be a danger for adults. And even though any given person truly feels like they will not be the one – every individual can now say they have had at least one family member affected in some way by Cancer.

These unspoken truths are consistent world-wide and they are statements that are not anything new or unknown. But what is new and unknown - even seemingly to the church today - is the power and authority we (Believers) have over our own bodies, our own health and most importantly, the health of the church collectively.

Within the membership of any individual church today, you will find a multitude of physical ailments, pains, sicknesses, illnesses, weaknesses, diseases, disorders, addictions and even birth defects or deformities. Add these to the underlying spiritual, psychological and/or emotional issues that are the source of our problems, and ultimately there is an enormous and epidemic need for healing in every church!

In fact, it is probably safe to say that nearly every adult member in most Christian churches today are in need of some kind of healing, salvation or deliverance – and that includes the pastors and leaders! And unfortunately, when church leaders are unhealthy, the teaching regarding healing is unhealthy, stemming more from experience than the saving word of God.

It has been said that a person doesn't change until first they are desperate enough to prepare; then prepared enough to do it. And sometimes it is the leadership that has the largest difficulty with change!

A new Believer might be wide-eyed and hungry, eager to believe the Word of God for healing, and therefore, they can be more receptive towards being healed. But as "mature" Christians who have been saved for a while; preaching for a while and Pastoring their congregations for a long time; we may tend to feel as if we should know better; that we should be further along in our faith or that we know all there is to know about healing already. And therefore, when the Church body hasn't received healing individually or collectively, we tend to make excuses and justifications that provide answers, soothe our souls and seem to be right. But they still lead to death![43]

Just like the man by the pool of Bethesda, far too many of us get too comfortable in our man-made answers, experiential excuses, "religious" justifications, denominational doctrines and our own personal desperation. With these five "healing barriers" we are unprepared for healing to take place in our own bodies – let alone throughout our whole church.

And this is not too harsh of an assessment for the church today, especially when we look at the man from Bethesda in John 5:2-9. The situation was that, at a particular season of time, an angel would come to the pool of Bethesda and trouble the waters. The first one in would receive healing.

John 5:6-7

"When Jesus saw him [the man] lie, and knew that he had been now a long time in that case, he said unto him, Will you be made whole? The impotent man answered him, Sir, I have no man, when the water is troubled, to put me into the pool: but while I am coming, another steps down before me."

From these two passages of text we find all five healing barriers:

1. **Man-Made Answers**
    Jesus asked the man a "yes or no" question. But the man's answer came from his flesh and clearly wasn't based upon the truth of Jesus as Healer. He didn't know Jesus as the Healer and sadly, neither do many Christians today.

2. **Experiential Excuses**
    Instead of simply saying, "Yes, I want to be healed," the man gave Jesus excuses based upon his experience. It may have seemed legitimate, however; apparently the man had found someone willing to put him by the water in the first place, so his reasoning was instantly reduced to an excuse.

3. **Religious Justifications**
    A "religious justification" would be something that seems the right thing to do based upon your religious beliefs or something you do religiously. It was his belief that there was no other way for his healing than being into the water first. Therefore, he justified himself in not being healed.

4. **Denominational Doctrines**
    A "denominational doctrine" is a particular teaching held by a like-minded group of believers who congregate based upon their shared understanding of the teachings. And at the First Church Pool of Bethesda, the man and his fellow members all believed the same "angel" healing doctrine!

5. **Personal Desperation**
   Apparently, this man had once been desperate enough for healing so that he made enough change to get to the pool where healing was possible. However, Jesus could see he had been in that state a long time. His own personal desperation became a comfort zone that kept him from preparing for healing (by finding a man to put him in the water), and therefore, he hadn't been healed already.

We may tend to believe that the Church has evolved in our doctrines and belief since the times of the Bible. But honestly, that is not necessarily true – especially in the areas of healing. The five healing barriers that kept the man by the pool of Bethesda from being healed are the same hindrances that can block the "mature" Believer from being healed as well.

The man had been in impotent in his legs and feet for 38 years, hoping for healing for 38 years, and religiously following the same beliefs and practices with the same ineffective results for who knows how long… just like Christians.

How many of us have been sick for 38 years; 8 years or 8 months? How many of us have been hoping for healing for all the 38 years; 8 years or 8 months we've been Christians? And how many of us have followed the same teachings, doctrines and beliefs about healing for the 38 years; 8 years or 8 months we've been members of our church or denomination?

Well, just like the man from Bethesda – it doesn't matter how long or what our excuses are. Jesus is still the Healer and if you're prepared to be healed then He says "Get up, be healed!"

Believers who attend the "Global Christian Church" all over the world, in every denomination are sitting at their own "Pools of Bethesda." They come to church sick, hurting, desperate and in need to the place where healing can be received – where it has been rumored that healing can be found – but maybe only by the lucky or the few; by their own correctly calculated effort or perhaps by some supernatural, mystical chance that is devoid of understanding.

And yet year after year, week after week and day after day, the Children of God have become accustomed to their collective states of health; accepting of the comforting answers from the pulpit and settle in to a lifestyle of excuses, prayer and hope.

I have seen many Christians and unbelievers become disheartened and discouraged by the lack of healing in their own lives or the lives of loved ones and especially when the result was the loss of life.

In cases of Cancer, in particular, the individuals who were trusting in God, did everything the doctors told them; they did everything "right" and they did everything they were "supposed" to. And yet, death was still the outcome. The discouragement, disappointment and disbelief that ensued however, was not towards the doctors who were supposed to have had the tools to "fix," cure or remove the cancer, but towards God who apparently did not.

For all that we pray for and plead God for when a loved one suffers from sickness, we still misunderstand the tools we have.

A doctor takes great care to describe the illness or disease, they carefully explain the tools at their disposal to attempt to fight it and they will specifically outline the risks as well as the probabilities of success and the percentage of life expectancy. Finally, the doctor (primarily for their own protection) will make sure their patient knows there are absolutely no guarantees.

And when, true to their word, the healing, cure or fix that was not guaranteed, does not transpire, the direction of the discouragement is not pointed at the doctor, but towards God.

Church Weapons:

Workbook Question: Is your Church equipped to heal?

When our bodies are sick – and depending upon the sickness – we will discover that sickness in one of two ways. We'll either feel the symptoms in our bodies and seek medical treatment, or a routine visit to a doctor will reveal something that needs treating. Let's refer to that as the "front-end issue." The "back-end issue" then would be the actual treatment and/or medicine we take in order to cure or manage that disease or sickness in our bodies.

For most Christians – pastors, leaders and members alike – there is little to no biblical or spiritual front end or back end approach when it comes to sickness or even maintaining our health. Reading and believing the word regarding healing would be the front end action; while believing and applying the word of God by faith would be the back end solution.

Now, many, many Christians hear the word, but do not necessarily believe the word – therefore they cannot apply the word. These are Christians, leaders, pastors and church members who do not believe that healing is for today, or that it is God's will to heal or that healing is for them.

There are however, those Believers who go beyond the more common beliefs and teachings of today's Christianity and they actually do believe in healing for today - for the Christian, and for unbelievers - and that it is God's will to heal.

While many, if not most of these Believers will read and believe the Word on the front end, on the back end they have issues believing and applying the word – or in essence – receiving the healing they believe. We have to mix the Word we say we believe with faith that God <u>will</u> perform His Word![44]

This is the disconnect of belief that is reflected upon the majority of the church body. As individuals are suffering from disease and sickness in their bodies, their physical illness is "filtered" through their beliefs in the word, and then manifests in the church collectively. Because of this, we are still very much like the father whose son threw himself into the fire and the water.

Mark 9:24
"And straightway the father of the child cried out and said with tears, Lord, I believe; help my unbelief!"

It is very easy for Christians to believe and yet have an unbelief that blocks the very thing we say we believe! And, many of us are more acutely aware of what we do believe, more than we are of the unbelief that blocks our blessings. But Jesus answers us today with the same truth He gave that father then:

Mark 9:23
"Jesus said unto him, If you can believe, then all things are possible to him that believes!"

Belief is the force of power that adds fuel to the Word of God so that the combination is a faith that manifests the Word!

Say that again!

> **Belief added to the Word of God is the fuel that makes the kind of faith that will manifest the Word of God in every area of your life!**

Believing in healing seems so simple and we've covered much of it already, however, it cannot be reiterated enough.

Far too many Christians believe erroneously and those beliefs are perpetuated by our leaders. Every myth surrounding healing is another obstacle that the enemy uses to keep us from walking in total, divine health. And there are so many different ways in which we disbelieve in healing that, "disbelief" becomes the biggest hindrance to being healed.

- You have to believe the word of God. You cannot pick and choose or rewrite what you believe.
- You have to believe that it is God's will to heal. Wondering what "His will" is, will hinder your healing.
- You have to believe that God heals today – that healing was not just for "bible times" or Jesus' ministry.
- You have to believe that healing IS for you – no matter what. Don't limit whether or not God will heal you.
- You have to believe God does **not** punish you or teach you lessons through poor health or sickness.
- You have to believe that the Jesus in you heals the SAME as He did when He walked upon the earth.
- You have to believe that you have more spiritual control over your health and healing than **anyone** else.

Healing is not arbitrary. Getting healed does not happen by some cosmic roll of the dice as if God is playing Russian roulette with your health. God wants you well. God wants you whole. Why would God provide healing through Jesus 2000+ years ago, and then not want you to be healed today? It doesn't make sense! God is not picking and choosing who gets healed and why, or when. God anointed Jesus with Holy Ghost power to heal all who had a need. And Jesus is the same yesterday, today and forever.[45]

Jesus is the Healer. And so, that means if Jesus lives in you, then the Healer lives in you and His desire for your healing and the healing of others is the same as when He lived upon the earth. Jesus' desire, power, anointing and will for YOUR healing is the same as it was for all those multitudes of individuals he healed in His ministry. And not once did he ask them if they were worthy of healing or if they had sinned. Nor did He deny them healing because their illness was somehow punishment!

Yes, there are many of our experiences that quite frankly, don't make sense. It seems as if we can't always explain why Believers and their loved ones get sick or die before their time – especially when we are praying and begging God for their healing. But the truths of the Word God do not change because of our experiences. The Word of God may not always make sense, but it is intended to always make faith![46]

๏Church Solutions:

Workbook Question: Is your Church committed to healing?

Whether for your own body, your local church body or the entire body of Christ - the Church Universal – whether member or leader – we have all got to do three fundamental things for our healing:

1. Believe in healing.

2. Understand biblical healing

3. Take spiritual control of our overall health: body, soul & spirit as well as individually, collectively and universally as members of the body of Christ and witnesses unto Him upon the earth.

Now, biblically there are many different ways in which people received their healing. Most common is that Jesus laid hands on people. Most notable is the woman with the issue of blood who touched the hem of Jesus' garment. But in truth, there were multitudes also who touched the hem of his garment and received their healing. Most people were brought to Jesus, although He was willing to go to people. But in just a few cases, Jesus never had to go because the faith of the individuals brought about healing for someone else who was not in Jesus' presence.

Sometimes the multitude was so great that Jesus could not lay hands on them all and they received healing anyway through His preaching or perhaps just being in the vicinity of his divine virtue. Sometimes Jesus asked the people to do the impossible like stretch out a withered hand or walk on impotent crippled legs. Other times Jesus did the impossible to people like spitting and making mud to put on the eyes of the blind.

There was only one case of a blind person receiving their sight in which we might compare it to a "progressive" healing – but most healings happened instantly, suddenly or in that self-same hour. And even the so-called "progressive" healing was simply a few moments that consisted of "as they went" or "try again" and "now what do you see?"

Everyone who had a need received their healing, and there are only two biblical accounts in which that did not happen. The disciples couldn't heal the boy who was throwing himself in the fire and in the water. And in Jesus' own home town he could do no great miracles there. However, even still in both cases there were acts of healing. The disciples could not heal the boy, but Jesus did. And in his home town, scripture says, "only a few sick folk were healed."[47]

So what was the hold up? Unbelief. Jesus could do no great miracles in His hometown because of their unbelief.[48] And in the case of the father and his son, you might think it was the father's unbelief that hindered his son's healing – after all, when Jesus asked if he believed, he did say, "I believe, Lord, but help thou mine unbelief." The father admitted he had unbelief – but it was the unbelief of the disciples that hindered them from healing the boy. And when they'd asked flat out why they could not heal him, Jesus told them, "because of your unbelief – this kind comes out not but by prayer and fasting." [49]

Oh, traditional thought would have you thinking that the spirit vexing that boy was too strong for the disciples – but it was actually their own unbelief that was too strong for them to walk in the same authority of deliverance and healing that they had already been walking in!

CHURCH NOTE:
- *There is NO demon too "strong" for the Word of God, the power of the name of Jesus or the authority of an anointed Believer!*
- *Fasting and prayer does NOT build up any power over devils!*
- *Only unbelief has the ability to overcome or over-power faith and only prayer and fasting can cast out that kind of unbelief!*

When Jesus sent out the disciples, calling them Apostles and telling them to go preaching and teaching the Kingdom of God, healing the sick and casting out devils, that ability for them to do so came before Pentecost and before the power of the Holy Ghost descended upon them in the Upper Room. Jesus sent out the Apostles with the same tools he possessed to follow in the same example He'd witnessed unto them. You see, healing and deliverance were Jesus' greatest evangelistic tools. They were the tools he gave the disciples and it should be the tools we use as well.

Both accounts of healing circumstances that involved unbelief are actually the greatest clues as to the two categories of healing and even the effectiveness of both – in a way. You see, while there are many different biblical accounts of healing, and people were healed of many different things, there are really only two categories of healing: 1. Is the healing that is sought for someone else, and 2. Is the healing that is sought for ourselves. Now, there are two sub-categories as well, but you might be surprised to know how little they may actually have to do with whether or not healing is received.

The sub-categories of healing are sinner or unbeliever, and the Believer or Christian. So, both the sinner and the Believer can ask for healing for someone else, and both the unbeliever and the Believer can seek healing for themselves. The current day consensus however, seems to be that it is harder for a Believer to receive the miracle of healing. Why would that be if the Believer then is living in God's grace? This is where the two accounts of unbelief come into play. Let me lay it out specifically.

As I said before, healing was Jesus' greatest evangelistic tool. And most of the descriptions and instructions regarding healing are indeed explanations of healing as it pertains to someone else. A sinner is already an unbeliever by definition, right? And so the belief, or "the faith factor," resides then with the one who is doing the praying or declaring for healing. This lies in the example of the disciples who could not heal the son of the Father who admitted he had unbelief. When the disciples asked why they couldn't heal the boy, again, Jesus tells them it was due to their unbelief, and not the admitted unbelief of the father. In fact, when the father does admit that he had unbelief, Jesus doesn't launch into a faith sermon, then tell the father to repent of any leftover sin and then begin speaking in tongues for an hour or so. No, in fact, it seems as if Jesus ignores the issue of the father's unbelief and just goes ahead and heals the boy anyway.

Then in the account of Jesus' home town where just a few sick folk were healed, it seems as if these are the ones that came to or more accurately, would have come to Jesus themselves if they were not offended at Him and therefore, it was the unbelief of the ones that would not come for themselves that hindered their own healing.

You might think here in lies the issue with Believers being unable to receive their healing. From this account it may seem as if Christians have more unbelief regarding healing than sinners do. But the truth is, the unbelief of the unbeliever is so wide-open, so full and so complete that there are no "pre-conceived" notions to get in the way of the supernatural.

The key is in the word "unbelief." Unbelief is not, "not believing." Not believing is in the definition of the word "disbelief." Here's a way to think of it: dis-believe = don't believe, and un-belief is like "unmerited" or "unwarranted," "misguided" or "erroneous" belief.

The people from Jesus' own home town believed they knew Jesus already. Unbelievers also think they already have the answers about Jesus and who He is. But healing? They don't know what to think about that one way or the other! And unfortunately, many Believers think they know all there is to know about healing and Jesus as well, and therefore it is that erroneous and misguided "unbelief" that hinders their healing.

Mark 6:3 "Is not this the carpenter, the son of Mary, the brother of James, and Joses, and of Juda, and Simon? And are not his sisters here with us? And they were offended at him."

Their misguided, unmerited beliefs about Jesus are what the scriptures calls "unbelief." It was this unbelief that caused offense within them.

Likewise, both the disciples and the father of the boy with the spirit that threw him into the fire and into the water – both had unbelief. They believed in Jesus, but both had misguided, unwarranted beliefs about healing for the boy.

Mark 9:17-18 "And one of the multitude answered and said, Master, I have brought unto you my son, which has a dumb spirit; and wheresoever he takes him, he tears him: and he foams, and gnashes with his teeth, and pines away: and I spoke to your disciples that they should cast him out; and they could not."

The disciples saw the spirit tearing at the boy; foaming at the mouth and gnashing his teeth and they began to believe they could not cast this particular demon out – even though they had already been casting out evil spirits by the authority of the Lord. This unwarranted unbelief hindered their authority over the spirit that plagued this father's son.

But the father brought is unbelief to Jesus, crying out "Lord, I believe, but help thou my unbelief!"

Jesus' response: "if you can believe, all things are possible to them that believe," was backed up with the demonstration of belief, and the boy was healed.

The one thing that we can be absolutely sure was a catalyst for this boy's father having received healing for his son, is the very same thing that may be missing in many congregations that do not see healing among their members. This father was committed to change on behalf of his son!

In Mark 9:18, the father tells Jesus that he had brought his son to the disciples, but they could not heal the boy. This father could have given up then and there! After all, it had been a long time since his boy had been in that state – since he was a child in fact, implying that perhaps his son was now either a teen or a young man.

The disciples could have been this father's last ditch effort – and he too could have given up in the same unbelief that the disciples experienced upon seeing the spirit tear at his boy yet again, falling to the ground, wallowing and foaming at the mouth.

But no, this father was committed to seeing his son be healed and he continued in pursuit of Jesus – faith waning, and yet determined to not give up.

How many Believers, leaders or churches can say the same?! We must be committed to the Word of God and the belief that Jesus is a Healer still today – never giving up until our experience completely example the manifest truth of His Word!

Church Cure:

Workbook Question: Is your Church contagious to all?

Matthew 4:24
"And [Jesus'] fame went throughout all Syria: and they brought unto him all sick people that were taken with divers diseases and torments, and those which were possessed with devils, and those which were lunatic, and those that had the palsy; and he healed them all."

With all the war; strife and devastation in Syria these recently past years, I would that the fame of Jesus would be spread throughout all that region once again! But if we were to look at the Syria in this passage as if it were the "First Church of Syria," we cannot deny that the full congregation was walking in healing, deliverance and wholeness!

But Syria wasn't the only region affected by Jesus. Mark 9:35 says He "went about all the cities and villages, teaching in their synagogues, and preaching the gospel of the kingdom, and healing every sickness and every disease among the people." And Luke 9:6 says Jesus and the disciples "went through the towns, preaching the gospel, and healing everywhere."

If we were to look at all these cities, villages and towns as if they were our local congregations today, then the Church in Nazareth is a prime example of many churches in every city, town, village and country who seemingly hear the same gospel of the Kingdom, but do not receive, accept or see the same healing results!

Even in Galilee, which was the region surrounding Nazareth, Jesus went about "teaching in their synagogues, and preaching the gospel of the kingdom, and healing all manner of sickness and all manner of disease among the people." But none of these cities were infectious enough to ignite a healing out-break in Jesus' own home town!

By that same token, Nazareth wasn't infectious enough in their own unbelief to infect the neighboring towns either!

So often as pastors, leaders and members – we are taught not to (and perhaps really try not to) compare ourselves to other churches – especially in the areas of growth, membership and prosperity. But in terms of healing, it might be time to open our eyes and compare, especially if we lead or attend a church that does not walk in the healing beliefs or results as other churches in our "own home towns."

In California there are two neighboring cities in which one is a small, insignificant rural area, and the other is larger, more well-known, progressive and metropolitan. Of the two, the smaller one has many local churches in a variety of denominations with few non-denominational and/or "charismatic" congregations. There are very few churches, if any, in which the leaders or members cultivate a healing culture or belief structure.

In the larger, neighboring city, there are many, many denominational churches and many more non-denominational churches as well, including several well-known "mega" churches and at least one global congregation that oversees an international fellowship and whose pastors and affiliates are often seen on a variety of global Christian programming.

The gifts of healing, beliefs in healing and the various, and effective healing ministries among Christians in the bigger city are undeniably prevalent and extraordinary!

CHURCH NOTE:

Whatever your church's beliefs are, they are infectious and contagious! The health of your city depends on the health of your church. The health of your church depends on the health of your members, and the health of the members depends on the health of your leadership! Be contagiously healthy to the body of Christ!

Like in economics, there is a "trickle-down" theory at work in the Theology and doctrines of our churches. Yes, God can and will use any one to bless His Kingdom. Noah was a drunk; Abraham was a liar; King David was an adulterer and a murderer; and poor Gideon was basically just a "nobody."

The list goes on and on, even into the New Testament, from Rehab to Paul – everyone had issues! And in our ministries today I have seen people walking in sin usher in the presence of the Holy Spirit; diabetics saving souls from the behind the pulpit and obese individuals laying on hands to facilitate the healing of others!

But of course, this is not God's best for us! And as leaders, we are responsible for so much more than simply "setting a good example, and trying to do our best."

As the "angel" over our various churches,[50] the pastor's anointing trickles down to the congregation like the oil down Aaron's beard.[51] Pastors are the Old Testament priests of their churches – and the people were the reflection of the priest, not the other way around.

It is the responsibility of the Pastor to walk in divine health and healing for the benefit of their members. But quite often, it is the pastor who is overwhelmed, hard-working, pulled from every angle and devoid of any time or inkling to care for themselves! Even as simply an example to their congregations this is unacceptable!

However and unfortunately, it is the prevailing spirit of poor health that plagues an unhealthy pastor that will also have jurisdiction over the congregants. The same is true for a reasonably healthy pastor that has a "spirit of unbelief" regarding healing as well.

The health and well-being of every Christian is dependent upon the teachings they receive and the healing culture of their church. But that's not enough. Christian health reveals that the spiritual cure we need must begin at the top and be contagious enough to infect the whole body of Christ!

Say that again!

The Spiritual cure Christians need must start at the top of Christian leadership and be contagious enough to infect the whole body of Christ!

In the natural, it is not uncommon that the most effective treatments against various diseases are deemed as "experimental and risky." This is one aspect of the world regarding healing that the church might just need to imitate!

Yes, it is extremely risky to step out on faith for the healing of an entire church membership. And many leaders with successful healing ministries have testimonies of the many who were not healed in the beginning. But, they did begin! It is time for some (old) new beginnings in the church today!

Chapter Summary

- Christians suffer from the same sicknesses of the world.

- Christians must change their beliefs to receive healing.

- The Church is hindered by more "unbelief" than sinners.

- Leadership health is key toward congregational health.

DETERMINATION: Churches must believe differently than the world, in order to not only see different results than the world, but also to be able to affect healing and change in the world.

Church Work Book
CHAPTER 5, LESSON 5

Each question has several multiple-choice statements. Rate each statement with an answer from 1-5. "1" = not at all; "5" = frequently. Add your answers and find the results on page 142.

1. **Is your Church prepared for healing?**
   a. We hope for healing as it is God's will
   b. We pray and leave the results up to God
   c. Our pastor teaches on healing frequently
   d. Members minister healing to each other

2. **Is your Church equipped to heal?**
   a. We believe that only Jesus is the Healer
   b. Sometimes our pastor will pray for healing
   c. We have prayer for healing at every service
   d. Our Elders are anointed healing ministers

3. **Is your Church committed to change?**
   a. We are satisfied with our healing beliefs
   b. We trust in God's Sovereignty for healing
   c. We actively pursue healing for others
   d. We thank God for His gifts of healing to us

4. **Is your Church contagious?**
   a. Our community rarely sees healing miracles
   b. We see other churches experiencing healing
   c. Our healing beliefs are unique from others
   d. We send healing teams into the community

Note: Each section has a possible rating ratio of 4-20 pts
Each chapter lesson has a possible rating ratio of 16-80 pts

The Whole Body

HEALING THE INDIVIDUAL CHURCH

✎Church Growth:

Workbook Question: Will your Church survive?

Our personal health and the faith we have for healing become a part of the church congregation we belong to. The individual health of 30, 60, 100, 300, 3000 or 30,000 members, becomes the prevailing health climate of that particular church. Regardless of the leadership's own personal beliefs regarding healing, if they are not actively teaching healing and diligently establishing a culture that pursues healing among the members, that church can easily become imprisoned in a stronghold of sickness and disease, as individual members silently succumb to their own health issues. And the spirits of unbelief are just as pervasive and territorial as any spirit of infirmity – or death.

I once was in a church for a duration of time that (unbeknownst to me at the time), was a place of assignment for various spirits of bitterness, criticism and disapproval, and a spirit of infirmity as well. These spirits were very territorial and I was immediately attacked from all sides. Initially the attacks were easy to fend off spiritually, through prayer and the spoken word of God. However, as the attacks went on and became more frequent, they had a kind of "Chinese Water Torture" effect on me, and ultimately, because there were so many attacks, it became easy to give in to the "smaller" seemingly insignificant ones. But once I did, it opened the flood gates for the stronger attacks to come in and gain a foothold into my health and spiritual well-being.

Since the beginning of my call to the ministry, I'd had significant revelations regarding healing for my own body and for others. I had been able to grasp certain truths that became the ammunition I relied on to eradicate common colds; flus and allergies from my life; to alleviate new issues that cropped up; and to completely change the course of on-going issues that had plagued me as far back as high school! Galatians became my primary weapon of choice, in particular:

> *Galatians 3:13*
> *"Christ has redeemed us from the curse of the law, being made a curse for us: for it is written, Cursed is every one that hangs on a tree:"*

I knew that pain and sickness were part of "Earth Curse Package" that Adam and Eve bought for all mankind when they believed the lies of satan in the Garden! But through Jesus we are redeemed from every curse of the Law and every consequence of those curses as well! Realizing that every pain, every sickness, illness and symptom of a system in my body that refused to work "decently and in order," was a curse of the enemy made it easy for me to cry out, "I am redeemed"[52] over it all – and my body responded – not always right away, but always.

However, once I was attacked from all sides, it was clear – none of my previously effective "tricks" and truths were working as usual! I was no longer thriving in divine health, and for a long period of time - well after having left the territorial source of my attack – I was simply surviving from one issue through to the next. In desperation I had to look outside of Galatians and found that each of my 12 physical attacks was related to various spiritual truths in the Word of God – the majority were found in Ephesians.

As I studied the "Whole Armor of God," it was clear that each spiritual truth was to provide physical healing for my own body, but soon I realized that each aspect of the "armor" was also intrinsically linked with the healing of the Church as a whole.

It was in trying to understand why my "normal" attempts and declarations of healing were not working that God revealed to me that as: "All things work together for the good of them that love the Lord and are the called according to His purpose,"[53] it was to His purpose that my growth and new understandings related to the healing I needed, would be a benefit to his people, and ultimately to anyone within the full church body who would receive it. So that now, through the research and construction of these in-depth studies, I have been able to see my own physical issues as a window of enlightenment for the plight and life of the church today. And as I "go through" I pray it leads others to the other side of their afflictions and challenges into the success and prosperity of their physical health as well![54]

The Global, Western and Progressive church has for far too long, simply attempted to survive their health issues (as well as many other kinds of issues), in the same manner as the world and through the same resources.

The church however, has always been meant to provide the world with the Kingdom solutions to these problems just as Jesus did as He went about from every city and village, healing all who had a need.

This is how the Kingdom of God will truly be built. As each person who is called and purposed by God through Jesus Christ matures in their own growth and thrives in their own divine health, the church body will reflect the people who comprise it. Then, as the world sees the Church thriving and prospering, they will be drawn to the answers that only Jesus can provide!

✒Church Increase:

Workbook Question: Will your Church thrive?

The attacks to my health that I endured were a direct result of me having come under the territorial jurisdiction of the spirits of sickness and infirmity that plagued that church. But the source of those spirits being able to gain authority in that congregation and throughout its members in the first place – long before I got there - was largely due to the lack of an accurate understanding of healing today, and the absence of a healing culture strong enough to counter-attack and cast out those spirits!

The primary truth to understand is that - for most people – their physical health issues and deterioration is usually related to emotional or soul related issues. As leadership learns to identify these experiences in the Church today they can then relate them to scripture and apply them directly to very nearly "any" circumstance that plagues the health of their members.

As previously stated, our whole body is outlined in seven categories throughout Ephesians 6:11-18. The full list of my own "head to heel" attacks fit into those categories outlined in Ephesians as well. But these verses also offer us clues as to the spiritual remedies God has given for us to counteract them. Here is a reminder of the text:

Ephesians 4:14-18

"Stand therefore, having your (1) loins girt about with truth, and having on the (2) breastplate of righteousness; And your (3) feet shod with the preparation of the gospel of peace; Above all, (4) taking the shield of faith, wherewith you shall be able to quench all the fiery darts of the wicked. And take the (5) helmet of salvation, and the (6) sword of the Spirit, which is the word of God: (7) Praying always with all prayer and supplication in the Spirit, and watching thereunto with all perseverance and supplication for all saints;"

As we align the verses from Ephesians with the various physical attacks most commonly faced, we can see the deeper, underlying issues within the church that keep the predominate church body from increasing and thriving in God's purpose:

1. Loins -- A high rate of people are detrimentally harassed by severe bowel issues and reproductive issues. Therefore:
   a. The Church is constipated – unable to flow with the Spirit of God and move past sin and temptation.
   b. The Church is unproductive and unable to reproduce without struggle, pain and labor!

2. Breastplate – Heart disease is still the number one source of deaths in the United States. Therefore:
    a. The Church is not loving the Lord with all her heart. Her love is split with the love of the world; family, social issues and politics.
    b. The Church is not cleansed by the blood of Jesus and there are no testimonies of overcoming by the blood of Jesus. Her blood flow is blocked!
3. Feet Shod: Bone Spurs; Plantar Fasciitis and Varicose Veins are just a few of the common maladies suffered in the feet and legs. Therefore:
    a. The Church is not walking in unity of faith or belief. How can two walk together, less they agree? [55]
    b. The Church is marred with blemishes, bruises and even a cancer of internal corruption and unrighteousness. Our walk is tarnished because of the direction of our choices and behaviors.
4. Arm/Hand: Tendonitis; Ganglions and "Tennis Elbow" are now common ailments – including arthritis of the joints in the hands and feet. Therefore:
    a. If our hands represent giving, the Church has a closed fist – not just financially, but in love, kindness, forgiveness and the fruit of the Spirit.
    b. Our right arm represents strength, and the Church is weak. Conversely, our left arm represents prosperity and the church is either poor or poorly stewarding her wealth for the benefit of the world and the lost.
5. Head/Neck: Debilitating Migraine headaches now hinder a majority of adults and children too. Therefore:
    a. The Church is "inflamed" with pride, conceit and materialism that stifle truth and revelation.

6. Mouth/Teeth: Despite the preventative measures in dental care, insurance and affordability still keep people suffering from a number of hugely detrimental dental issues, including root canals and Gingivitis. Therefore:
   a. The Church is not keeping the Word of God in their mouths and it is being affected by that which is abundant in their hearts. [56]
   b. And, the Church has not departed from the Corrupt Communications of the old man. Her mouth spews both fresh and bitter water. [57]
7. Prayer and Supplication: And finally, Depression of all kinds has reached epidemic highs in people of all ages and walks of life! Therefore:
   a. The Church is not walking in the 2 Timothy 1:7 understanding that God has not given us the spirit of fear, but of power and of love and a sound mind!

With all these things going on within any given church - sometimes every single one of them at once or reoccurring in the same time frame - it is no wonder that Christians frequently battle cases of depression; issues with bitterness as a result of unforgiveness; confusion and a deep sense of loss and grief as well. And because most people are so caught up in trying to simply manage their lives, they are unaware of their true states of mind, and therefore also unaware of the affects it has on their faith and prayer life.

So while, prayer may be the last thing listed in the Ephesians list of our Whole Armor, it often is the first target of the enemy, that, like a defense system, barricade or protective wall – once that system is weakened, it allows for all other areas to be hit, attacked and damaged as well.

When your prayer life suffers or has any weaknesses or gaps, it is one of the first ways in which the enemy can gain a foothold of poor health into your life. When the prayer life of your local congregation suffers, it is the very first way in which the enemy gains access into the health and life of your local church. And thereby, when many local churches suffer from gaps in their own collective and corporate prayers, the Church as a whole is again, sick, weak and ineffective.

It starts with prayer. Pastors need to pray for their members, just like individuals need to keep the overall health of their body covered in a general prayer of faith and belief in God's word for their healing.

This is KEY - not just for the individual as I've illustrated in my own example of attacks, but likewise this is key for the Church! Isaiah 56:7 says that God's house will be called a "house of prayer" but in the synoptic gospels of Matthew, Mark and Luke, Jesus is reported as saying that God's House of Prayer had been made a "den of thieves." Well, I don't know that Jesus would turn over tables for chicken dinners and raffle tickets but the truth is if there is an unhealthy church with many unhealthy members, the first point of entry in their lives individually and then collectively as a church is prayer – either the lack of prayer, praying ineffectual prayers, or being plagued by too much doubt so that the prayers are hindered. And please note, I did not say "unanswered." All prayer is answered but is it hindered?

Say that again!

ALL prayer is answered! And all the promises of God are answer yes and Amen![58] But maybe the unseen answers to your prayers are being hindered!

Matthew 20:16 says that the last shall be first and the first shall be last. I have found this biblical precept to be true in so many different areas of life. While prayer may be listed last – and in truth, some teachings do not even include prayer as a part of the Whole Armor of God – it must be the first area we look at to resolve any issue we face.

I think of prayer like a quiver of arrows, and the various types of arrows in that quiver are like the many different types of prayer we have at our disposal. One type of arrow may be ineffectual in one area of use but not another, whereas simply using a different arrow might get the job done more accurately. So that by knowing your arrows, you use them all to the best of what they were created for and therefore all your prayers accomplish what you send them out to do.

The enemy knows the potential power of our prayers better than we do. Even without knowing the various arrows of prayer at our disposal, or how to use them or what they're for -

a Believer who understands their own righteousness in Christ, can still accomplish much with any kind of prayer that's offered in pure faith at the right time.

> *James 5:16*
>
> *"Confess your faults one to another, and pray one for another, that you may be healed. The effectual fervent prayer of a righteous man avails much."*

Do not misunderstand this verse as many teachings do! Unfortunately, many in church leadership teach a "sin consciousness" that keeps members guilty and constantly confessing every sin they can think of and presumptuous sins they don't know they've committed as well! That is an erroneous understanding of this verse that literally keeps an Believer steeped in their sin and temptation rather than strengthened to walk free from them!

James 5:16 says to confess our faults – that is, our errors, mistakes and lapses in judgment. Between Believers, Christians and church members, this is an act of forgiveness within the church body, that when utilized correctly, it keeps unforgiveness from hindering us when we stand praying![59]

The devil knows better than we do that the prayers of a Christian will avail much and therefore, the enemy will attack us at our source of prayer first. And remember, that which is one person's condition individually is added to another's until collectively the whole church body suffers – with several ailments flaring up at once. While some members suffer from one thing, other members suffer from something else and soon the whole church body is suffering, miserable and ineffectual.

CHURCH NOTE:
Keeping your church suffering, miserable and ineffectual is how the enemy enacts his John 10:10 desire to "steal, kill and destroy" against the body of Christ. The enemy and all our battles are real!

It is intended by God that as the pastor preaches; the teachers teach and the elders lay hands on and pray healing for individuals, the spirits of lack and infirmity are cast out and members then testify how they have overcome by the blood of the lamb. And thereby as each individual member of the church body receives healing, the whole church is made whole as well. People outside of the membership are then drawn to the church for their own healing. And as the church increases in health; the church body grows, and Christians mature in their understanding and personal power against the enemy!

This is the culture of healing intended for each local church as it relates to the culture set by their leaders and members. Unfortunately, this structure is not understood; believed or even recognized in most cases. In fact, even among leaders who are anointed with gifts of healing there is often a lack of healing, growth and increase in their congregations![60]

❧Church Harvest:

Workbook Question: Will your Church bear fruit?

When a tree is healthy and its roots grow deep in an unending source of plentiful water, it will increase, grow strong and bear much fruit. If each church would be a tree, planted by the rivers of the Tree of Life, then the fruit resulting from their healthy healing beliefs and practices would be abundant!

Jesus is our Living Water[61] and we, as the church are cleansed by the washing of the water of His Word.[62] So then, at the end of all that is said, done, taught, spoken, prayed for and believed; why do Christians who have Jesus abiding within them, and the loved ones they prayer for, still suffer, get sick and die before their time and from the same circumstances as everyone else?

The question still seems to remain, permeate and consume our whole Christian existence: If we are supposed to be different than the world, why are we still exactly the same? What's that old saying? "If it looks like a duck; quacks like a duck and acts like a duck… It must be a duck." So, is the church just a lame duck? To the world, that's how we look – ineffectual and lame, suffering from the same hell as everybody else!

Matthew 16:18

"And I say also unto you, That you are Peter, and upon this rock I will build my church; and the gates of hell shall not prevail against it."

Yes, through Jesus and belief in Him we are now His church. But I like this old Southern wisdom that says: "You can raise kittens in an oven, but that don't make them biscuits!"

In other words, just because Christians have accepted Jesus and attend a church, doesn't mean they are conformed into the image of Jesus, or that have learned how to BE the church that the gates of hell cannot not prevail against!

John 15:7-8

If you abide in me, and my words abide in you, you shall ask what you will, and it shall be done unto you. Herein is my Father glorified, that you bear much fruit; so shall you be my disciples.

Whether ducks or kittens, abiding in Christ so that His words abide in us, is the very way in which we are conformed into His image as it says in Romans 8:29. However, Believers cannot and will not be conformed into the image of the Word of God if they are not being taught it accurately or do not believe in it because they compare the Word with their experiences.

Consequently, Christians sit in churches like sick and lame ducks or demure, helpless kittens, when they should be like biscuits: hot, miniature representations of the Bread of Life!

Believers are Christians who don't know how to be "Christ-like;" we learn doctrine without learning to be disciples; and we go to church, belong to churches and have wonderful church services without ever learning how to BE the Church and therefore, bear fruit and glorify God as Jesus intended for us to.

John 15:2

"Every branch in me that bears not fruit he takes away: and every branch that bears fruit, he purges it, that it may bring forth more fruit."

It's easy for Christians to be burdened by this verse. Like many other well-known verses in the word of God, our lack of knowledge as to the background and definitions behind the Hebrew and Greek leave us (understandably so) with our own limited Western English "translations" of what is written.

Therefore most of us are taught that John 15:2 is telling us that if Christians are not producing the fruit of the Spirit[63] in our lives, that we run the risk that God will "take us away" or cast us out of the Kingdom to be burned in eternal hell-fire (John 15:6).

And while the fear of hell can be an effective tool that has worked for centuries to convert sinners into Believers, it is not a threat of "reality" that applies to Christians once we have accepted Jesus and are actually "in Him" as the verses in John chapter 15 describe. The actual background truth of this verse however, is one that many pastors, leaders and members just do know, and have no reason to know otherwise.

If you were the husbandmen of a vineyard in Jesus' day and a vine from a branch of your grape plant was on the ground, it would not be able to bear any fruit. Therefore, you would pick up that branch and lay it across a trellis of sorts. The branch comes up from the ground and the vines are laid across the trellis in the shape of a capital "T." The English translation of the Greek phrase describing this action is "to take away," or "to bear away." And any vine that remains on the ground will eventually wither and die of its own so that the husbandman must then cut it off and will throw it into the fire to be burned.

As Christians in Christ, if we are not bearing the fruit of the Word of God in our lives, God will gently lift us up higher in our understanding so that we can bear fruit – that is His intention in regard to the Believer who has an unproductive and unfruitful understanding of healing.

The churches then, who have members with a desire for healing and Pastors and leaders who will indeed pray for healing are bearing some fruit, but John 15:2 is saying, God will "purge" or cut away the leaves of your erroneous understanding or unbelief that are dry, brittle and dying so that they do not zap the nutrients of truth out of your ability to bear much fruit!

Christians in churches with limited or no healing culture are not in danger of being cast way because they are not bearing fruit. No matter what fruit is in limited production, God will always try to get His truth to his people, as it is His intention that we walk in the fullness of His abundance!

Instead, far too many Christians and Churches are being "cast away" – not by God but through their own lack of knowledge (Hosea 4:6). And consequently, Believers who should be reaping the harvest of God's blessings, prosperity and good health[64] are instead suffering from and dying from the same sicknesses, diseases and ailments as the world.

∽Church Abundance:

Workbook Question: Will your Church Overflow?

In leadership – whether in the marketplace or in the ministry – it is commonly understood that if you've got a complaint, it's better received when you offer up a solution along with it!

Such is the case with all I've outlined regarding the state of healing among church communities; church leaders and Christians in relation to the world and their world-view of the church body in general.

If you are suffering from illness in your body – whether leader or member; if your church is largely unhealthy, plagued with sicknesses or perhaps dying out; and if your leadership has not expressed the same teachings on healing as have been outlined so far – do not be distressed! We serve a loving, patient, awesome God who wants nothing but His best for His kids!

It is already too easy for Christians to feel as if sickness was somehow a punishment from God for our sins – so, we do not need to add to that misplaced guilt and condemnation by feeling as if a lack of healing or unbelief in our lives or churches is in some way contributing to our poor health! Never forget, bad things come from a bad devil! We can and should only expect good from our good, good heavenly Father! And the good he wants us to expect is the goodness of His abundance and the overflow of all His promises!

Say that again!

Our good, good God and Heavenly Father wants us to expect only the goodness of His abundance and the overflow of all His promises to us!

We know that John 10:10 tells us that Jesus came that we might have life and life more abundantly, but still we have difficulty comprehending the fullness of abundance that God really does have for us. Unfortunately, we feel too unworthy of God's great grace for our lives and will disqualify ourselves from the overflowing expression of His love through our healing!

Ephesians 3:20
"Now unto him that is able to do exceeding
abundantly above all that we ask or think,
according to the power that works in us,"

God wants to work His healing power in us, if we'll let Him! Our churches can thrive in the exceeding abundantly above all we've currently been asking or thinking in regards to our health and healing! That's overflow! And in regards to our healing, overflow means that as we are healed we can heal others as well.

In Matthew chapter 10, Jesus sent out His newly commissioned Apostles to do as He had been exampling to them. He sends them out to "preach, saying, the kingdom of heaven is at hand. Heal the sick, cleanse the lepers, raise the dead, cast out devils." And at the end of it He admonishes them – "freely you have received, freely give." (Verse 8)

This is the overflow mind-set that every healthy church with a strong healing ministry should strive towards. All of God's promises – salvation, deliverance, prosperity, joy and healing – are not just simply meant to come to us, but through us to the benefit of the world!

Truthfully though, the world's persecution of the church has gotten so much worse in the last several years – and much of it is blatant and malicious. But not all if it is unwarranted.

In many cases, the church has brought it on upon herself, and self-professed Christians are not walking in the love that Jesus says will show the world that we are of Him! [65]

Imagine however, if Christians were no longer harsh and judgmental, but accepting and tender? What if instead of identifying the sins of others, we lived as if we knew we were made to be dead to sin because of the Righteousness of Christ? And instead of trying to create legislation that forced the world to live like Christians, Christians loved up on the world and provided solutions to their problems through the Word of God?

I think that would look like a church that was prospering through the abundance of their members – members who were prospering from the blessings they receive by being a blessing. [66]

It is a church that is healed, healthy and favored, sharing the overflow of all their blessings with the rest of the world. That is the church of Jesus that God intends for us to be!

Chapter Summary

- God's Word provides all the healing the church needs.

- Prayer is essential to the healing culture of the church.

- Christians abiding in Jesus will bear the fruit of healing.

- Healing abundance should be shared with the world.

DETERMINATION: When church members are conformed into the image of Jesus, abide in His blessings and rightfully receive their healing, the world's perspective of the church will change!

Church Work Book
CHAPTER 6, LESSON 6

Each question has several multiple-choice statements. Rate each statement with an answer from 1-5. "1" = not at all; "5" = frequently. Add your answers and find the results on page 143.

1. **Will your Church survive?**
   a. We know God will keep us until His return
   b. We do the best we can to do His will
   c. We know the word of God is our weapon
   d. We regularly advance on the gates of hell!

2. **Will your Church thrive?**
   a. We strive to be content in all things
   b. God's grace is sufficient for all our needs
   c. God is faithful to richly supply our needs
   d. God is the God of "more than enough!"

3. **Will your Church bear fruit?**
   a. We can do nothing of our own selves
   b. We try to walk in the Fruit of the Spirit
   c. We know pruning is sometimes painful
   d. We are blessed and give of all our blessings

4. **Will your Church overflow?**
   a. God doesn't promise to give what you want
   b. We have all provision in our righteousness
   c. We expect the open windows of heaven
   d. Our pastor has told us to stop giving before!

Note: Each section has a possible rating ratio of 4-20 pts
Each chapter lesson has a possible rating ratio of 16-80 pts

1

The Whole Church

HEALING THE WHOLE BODY OF CHRIST

∞Church Elements:

Workbook Question: Does your Church receive healing through Communion?

A new controversy in the church today is the idea that healing can be received through the communion elements. Actually, it is amazing to me that if there is to be any controversy surrounding communion, that it hasn't been regarding the teachings that communion is only for Believers, or that anyone with sin in their life must first examine themselves to determine whether they are worthy enough to partake.

Without launching into an entirely unrelated topic, it is necessary to dispel these "myths" in order that churches today might receive the full benefit of just exactly what Jesus has given to us through this ritual of breaking bread and the cup of His blood.

Communion Myth #1:

Every Christian knows that John 3:16 says if we believe on Jesus we shall have everlasting life. But did you know that John 6:54 says the same about Communion?

"Whosoever eats my flesh, and drinks my blood, has eternal life; and I will raise him up at the last day."

We know that "whosoever" applies to whomever is a sinner that believes on Him, because you and I were included in that sentence when we confessed Jesus as our Lord and Savior. By that same truth, "whosoever" applies to the whatever sinner believes that taking of the bread and drinking of the cup will give them eternal life as well.

Oh, we can try to add, "Yes but – the must repent, and examine themselves and so on and so on," but we don't go on and on like that when it comes to the simple act of salvation offered through belief in John 3:16.

Communion Myth #2:

Every Christian knows that we are all just "sinners saved by grace" and that we have all "sinned and fallen short of the Glory of the Lord."

We are all, always, unworthy of the grace we've been given through Jesus Christ. Yes, we are now saved, forgiven and given new life in Christ that we can live dead to sin, and God chooses not to remember our sins – past, present and future.

But if we all are going to be honest and examine ourselves our grace and righteousness is unearned and therefore is not ours due to our efforts. Our efforts still deem us as unworthy, and therefore if we base are partaking on what we examine in ourselves, none of us should ever be allowed to partake in communion – saved or unsaved.

Communion Myth #3:

Some ministers (famous ones at that) would have us to believe that if we do examine ourselves to have sin in our life and we still partake of communion, we are taking "unworthily" and will "eat and drink damnation unto ourselves."

Clearly this is related to the previous myth. If we determine that our own standards of examination supersede God's then we all will inadvertently eat and drink damnation to ourselves. Therefore, we have to logically conclude that God must be saying something else here when it comes to partaking unworthily or eating and drinking damnation unto ourselves. It is this last myth that is directly related to whether or not healing is available through communion.

Before we go on to look at the entire passage, be sure to know that by highlighting and even exposing the myths surrounding communion, I am in no way minimizing the supernatural significance or sanctity of this aspect of our Christianity that we are told to do as "often as we do." I believe communion is a Holy expression of Jesus' great exchange for us.

1 Corinthians 11:23-30

"*For I have received of the Lord that which also I delivered unto you, That the Lord Jesus the same night in which he was betrayed took bread: And when he had given thanks, he brake it, and said, Take, eat: this is my body, which is broken for you: this do in remembrance of me. After the same manner also he took the cup, when he had supped, saying, This cup is the new testament in my blood: this do, as oft as you drink it, in remembrance of me. For as often as you eat this bread, and drink this cup, you do show the Lord's death till he come. Wherefore whosoever shall eat this bread, and drink this cup of the Lord, unworthily, shall be guilty of the body and blood of the Lord. But let a man examine himself, and so let him eat of that bread, and drink of that cup. For he that eats and drinks unworthily, eats and drinks damnation to himself, not discerning the Lord's body. For this cause many are weak and sickly among you, and many sleep.*"

We have been given communion by Jesus as a representation of what His body did for us on the cross and what His blood does for our redemption from sin. This we know and do in remembrance of Him. However, while the church in Corinth misunderstood communion and did so as a form of fellowship and were getting drunk, or were partaking as if it was the evening meal, we too have misunderstood communion in an opposite extreme.

We read and teach from these passages and use them to judge, condemn and chastise one another – even though verses 31 and 32 warn us not to. And yet for generations and even at a Sunday service in the early part of 2015 I have heard preachers and deacons admonishing the congregation to be careful not to "take communion unworthily, lest they bring damnation upon themselves. And to examine themselves before partaking to see if they have ought against anyone (or that anyone has ought against them) that must be resolved before they take communion."

What a load of mixed up, misunderstood hogwash! Verses 23-30 in 1 Corinthians 11 is telling us that we take communion unworthily if we **do not discern the Lord's body**. And, the damnation or condemnation we bring upon ourselves comes also from **not discerning the Lord's body.** And how does that condemnation or damnation reveal itself in us? Verse 30 says **THIS** is the reason many of you are sick, weak and sleep (die). Not discerning the Lord's body is the reason many of us get sick, are weak and powerless, suffering from many strength debilitating illnesses like depressions and fibro myalgia or die from any number of diseases.

Say that again!

Not discerning the Lord's body at communion is the reason many of us get sick, are weak and powerless or die before our time.

Don't shoot the messenger if you don't like the message, but that's what the Word of God says!

When we take communion, we always discern the Lord's blood. Jesus clearly says, "this cup is New Testament in my blood: which was shed for the remission of your sins." (Matthew 26:28) We know what Jesus' blood has done for us. We plead the blood of Jesus on everything from our house to our kids to our pets. We sing songs about the blood still works – because it does. And so, because we discern the blood of Jesus, we reap the benefits and eternal rewards of the blood of Jesus.

But because we neglect to consider, or out and out reject what the Lord's BODY has done for our body – we walk in condemnation and damnation and call it "getting old" or call it "diabetes" or call it "heart disease" or call it "tired all the time."

Sickness, disease, dis-ease and death are NOT of God – they are the weapons of the enemy. In fact, death is the last enemy of God still yet to be put under his feet![67] And if we were to learn how to discern the Lord's body and walk in the fullness of our salvation and in the benefits of communion, we would not be sick – because God sent his word and healed, [68] and by his stripes we are healed. [69] And we would not be weak because the weak would say I am strong and the poor would say I am rich! [70] And we would not perish until 120 years of age because that's how long God's spirit will tarry with us [71] – and like Moses we will pass from life to sleep and into eternal life and our eyes would not be dim nor our strength abated! [72]

All of these declarations are in the Word of God and they are the power of God's word for our lives! It is true that people – and even Believers who believe will still get sick, suffer weakness and lack, and even pass away. But when we believe the word of God and declare its truths, the very word of God will heal sickness; it will strengthen where we are weak; it will prosper where there is lack and it will raise again what has died!

ᨀ Church Essentials:

Workbook Question: Speak the Word of Truth?

So, what does it mean to "declare the truths of God?" When we declare or speak the word of God in absolute faith, the Word of God will speak life – even abundant life – to that which the devil is trying to steal, kill or destroy! Proverbs 18:21 says, "Death and life are in the power of the tongue: and they that love it shall eat the fruit thereof." And John 6:63 says "It is the spirit that quickens; the flesh profits nothing: the words that I speak unto you, they are spirit, and they are life."

Believers must believe the word of God. And when we speak that which we say we believe, we will see more health added to our flesh; our lives; and the life of the entire church body. Out of the abundance of the heart the mouth speaks!

CHURCH NOTE:

It is absolutely essential that the Church speak the Word of God!
- Hearing and hearing the Word increases faith for the Word.
- Declaring the Word in faith, manifests the Word!
- The manifest Word of God increases the manifest power of God!

Pastors must set the example of declaring the Word of God outside of that which is spoken during a Sunday sermon, "turn to your neighbor" statement! If pastors are teaching healing truths, the must also make sure their congregations are believing those truths deep in their hearts. If the church does not deeply believe what is being taught, they will only mimic the words spoken, like a parrot with perfect pronunciation and no understanding.

Jesus spoke quite a few parables regarding "the seed" that the disciples simply did not understand. They begged Him to explain and he did so beginning with this simple statement:

> *Luke 8:11*
> *"Now the parable is this: The seed is the word of God."*

From this understanding of the Word of God, one parable in particular examples how the word works in our lives when we believe it and continue to speak from that which we believe.

Jesus says in Mark 4:26-27 that the Kingdom of God is like a man that casts seed into the ground. If the seed is the word, then the ground is our hearts and how we receive and believe the word of God. Then Jesus said that man would go to sleep, night and day until that seed would suddenly spring up, "he knows not how."

Well, I know how! Like the woman with the issue of blood who kept saying, "if I can but touch the hem of His garment, I know I shall be healed." Saying and saying and continuing to say, speak, meditate and declare the word of God will cause faith for that word to arise in your life, and when faith for that word arises, that manifestation of that word – whatever it is – will spring up in your life!

Too much of the scriptures tell us how much we should declare the word of God in order for the word to work – after all, it's been said that we live in a "voice activated system," because that's the system God used to create all of creation!

Job 22:28 says "we shall decree a thing and it shall be established and the light will shine upon our ways." And most powerful is Joshua 1:8 which tells us that meditating on the word and keeping it in your mouth is how we have good success and make our own way prosperous!

Any congregation that wants to experience good success, and make their own way prosperous – especially the 3 John 1:2 prosperity in health and soul – must do more declaring, decreeing, meditating and speaking the healing word of God!

✍Church Environment:

Workbook Question: Can your Church keep a healing culture?

I am convinced that there are too many scriptures regarding our healing and for the health and wellness of our bodies for anyone to not believe in healing. But all too often Christians believe in their experiences rather than believe the truth. And pastors feel it's safer to give Jesus an "out" and preach according to what they themselves can't explain.

But Jesus healed everyone who had a need and if we believe that Jesus was the healer, and believe that Jesus lives in us, then why can't we believe that Jesus still is the healer in us and through us? God is Jehovah Rophi – the Lord who heals. And when we learn the names of God we easily accept this right along with Malachi 3:6 that says, "I the Lord, change not..." or Hebrews 13:8 that says Jesus is the "same yesterday, today and forever." Why then do we think that God will no longer heal us today or that His word on healing no longer is for today, or that Jesus does not heal in the exact same ways and frequencies in which He healed when He walked the earth?

For healing to succeed within us individually and collectively, we as a people and as a church, must first realize, understand and believe without doubt or question several fundamental truths from God's word. In other words, for us to receive the truth of God's Word, we have to believe God's word is true. And if we believe that God's word is true, then we must accept that His truth applies to us today. That means we won't see God's truth for our healing until we believe in it. And so in order to establish and maintain a healing culture in our churches, and thereby see healing manifested through us into our families, communities and the nations, our leaders have got to commit to certain fundamental truths:

- Healing is for us today – all of us believers and sinners.
- It is God's will for us to be healed, with no exceptions.
- Sickness, disease, illness, pain and death are of the devil – no exceptions!
- God is not trying to teach us anything or get our attention through sickness.
- Death is never the answer of healing we are praying for
- Offence and unbelief *in Jesus as a healer for you or for today* can hinder your healing but not sin – never sin.
- Yes, God can use doctors for your healing, but that is not His ultimate best for you.
- God has already given us healing through Jesus' work on the cross 2000+ years ago.
- We cannot continue to ask God to give what He's already given and expect to see it.
- We have been given control over our own healing, the healing of our churches and the healing of our nations.[73]

For the sake of accurately conveying biblical truths regarding the connection between our individual healing, the healing of the church and the Word of God, it is imperative that the statements above are received as true. These are the very doubts that hinder God's people from accurately and consistently experiencing the kind of healing that would dispel these myths once and for all! It's an unending cycle of misunderstanding that must be rejected – like the brown, crispy, FLIMSY, outer skin of an onion - if we going to receive the layers of benefits God has for us as a people and church through His divine healing.

Sickness is a distraction that the enemy uses to keep a congregation and the church from growing. And, he will even use the pastor's teaching about sickness, health and divine healing to advance his purpose!

If an individual believer in the congregation is suffering in sickness and pain, they cannot hear the sermon messages that would help them grow in any area of their life. And, if that sickness causes damage in their finances, family peace, relationships, job, or any other area of life, then that person is hindered from growing in faith for God to work in any of these areas. Then, if the pastor teaches a doctrine that does not believe in healing, or does not help to grow true faith, then the enemy uses those errors from the pulpit to keep the whole church in bondage, in sickness and hindered from growth.

But most individuals and pastors do not realize that most of the teachings and prayers that acknowledge Jesus is our Healer can also be used to keep the congregation and the church in the bondages of sickness.

When the pastor establishes, promotes and teaches a healing culture and understanding that implies Jesus heals some of the time; that prayers for healing are answered sometimes yes, sometimes no or sometimes wait.; or that sickness is a way of God getting a person's attention – or even prays a prayer that begs, pleads and asks for healing from a perspective of hoping that God will grant a miracle of healing, then this pastor is setting a culture based upon human experience. And, all of these perspectives will be used by the enemy to keep the church sick and unhealed.

It is a "catch 22" of error that many if not most pastors and believers fall into. These types of understandings and teachings are based upon <u>experience</u>. They attempt to give peace and hope in areas where circumstances don't always turn out the way we hope, or the way we read in the Bible.

However, preaching from experience only ensures more of the same experiences that ultimately only validate and perpetuate the teaching that is based upon human experience!

Say that again!

Preaching from experience only ensures more of the same experiences that ultimately only validate and perpetuate the teachings based upon our experiences!

It is a trap of the enemy that is far too easy to fall into and without even realizing it. I have visited far too many churches in which the leadership and members have a strong heart for healing, but their words are as weak as their faith.

I have spoken on healing in far too many churches in which the members shouted and "amened" the message; the leadership spoke in seeming agreement and understanding when the surmised the message, but then turned right around and negated the message in the habit of their traditional "Altar Call" or closing prayer.

And I have spoken to far too many Christians who have acknowledged that God will heal them, but then cancel that probability by adding... "in His own time," or "if it is His will."

I cannot express it or teach it enough! Christians, leaders, pastors and members – we have to get tough! We must understand our authority in Jesus,[74] stand in our God-given dominion,[75] speak boldly in our faith,[76] walk in the power we've been given over all the powers of the enemy,[77] and command our own healing by telling the pain to go, telling all sickness to be plucked up from its root; and telling our bodies to comply to the word of the Lord! And instead of claiming disease by name, as in "my this" and "my that..." we should be calling that disease by name and telling it to bow unto the name of Jesus which is the name above every other name![78] And when praying for the healing of others, we don't need to shout or pray in tongues forever. As Commanders we have confidence in our authority!

∽Church Excellence:

Workbook Question: Can your Church be made whole?

Jesus is the Head of the Church and the Church is His body. God has seated Jesus at His right hand until all of His enemies are made His footstool. That means as His body we too are seated at the right hand of the Father. And as His body, the feet of Jesus are the feet of the Church! One by one the enemies of the Lord are being paraded before Christ and the Church and God is making each defeated enemy to bow down and prostrate themselves beneath the feet of the Church! [79]

If the Church Universal were to have a revelation of this truth today, it might look as if she was waiting for an appointed time – asking God, "When will you make our enemies our footstool? When will the Church be redeemed and delivered from the enemy of persecution; poverty; powerlessness, sickness and pain?"

The Whole Church has been waiting for so long that our waiting has become impatient – like a patient in the waiting room of the doctor's office, waiting on the prognosis of a biopsy. If the doctor waits too long, the patient can no longer sit in patience and will jump up, anxiously pacing and walking the floor, unable to rest, relax and receive the news with ease – positive that any news will be bad news!

The Church Universal is pacing the floor in these end times. We are anxiously awaiting the return of Jesus to rapture the Church and rescue us from all we've not been delivered from.

Churches throughout the whole body of Christ have jumped up on our collective feet; collectively suffering from the same ailments of the world, waiting to be delivered from them, and no longer expecting to conquer them or able to believe that Jesus has.

But like the king from a neighboring country that is conquered by the prevailing king – he is as defeated as are all of the churches enemies of sickness, disease, illness, pain and poor mental health – as well as fear, lack and other enemies as well.

> *Hebrews 10:12-13*
> *But this man [Jesus], after he had offered one sacrifice for sins forever, sat down on the right hand of God; From henceforth expecting till his enemies be made his footstool.*

If the prevailing king does not sit down, resting upon his throne, to pick up his feet for the conquered king to be placed beneath them, it does not matter who that conquered foe might be. The king must sit, the king must rest; the king must lift his feet so that he can place his feet on the backs of his enemies!

Likewise, even though Jesus has conquered every enemy of the church through the cross, the Church has got to sit, and rest, and lift her feet in order for God to put each enemy beneath us – including death.

Obviously the Church Universal isn't going to sit down collectively at the count of three! And neither will each local church. But when pastors teach their members to sit; to eat from the banquet table of His Word that He has prepared for us before our defeated enemies of lack, poverty, sickness, disease, pain, depression, illness and suffering in their individual churches, then individual people will begin to rest in the Lord.

One by one, as Christians learn to rest in the Lord (seated in Heavenly places in Christ Jesus), the rightly divided word of truth they are being fed will teach them to lift their feet. Lifting your feet for the Lord to make our enemies our footstool means Christians stop walking in their own direction; they will stop walking according to their own knowledge and understanding; they'll stop walking in the direction they think will get them to healing and deliverance, and they will let the Spirit of the Law of Life do the work for them.

And as each Christian sits down in their heavenly place; receiving the Spirit of Truth and pick up their feet of false teachings and self-effort – receiving God's promises into their lives and in their bodies; that's when the Christ defeated enemy of sickness will be make their footstool! And as more and more Christians rest and receive their healing; whole churches will have the enemy of healing to be made their footstool. And as each local church sits and rests in the finished work of Jesus, so will the entire Church body, the Church Universal.

Jesus will return for the whole Church – complete and entire. It will also be a Church made whole, healthy, healed and delivered. It will be a glorious church, without spot or wrinkle and without blemish![80]

This is the promise given to the Bride of Christ, His Church, the members of His body. It is through the blood of Jesus that God already sees the church as healed, whole, blemish-free and beautiful.

It is now time – passed the time, in fact - that through supernatural healing and divine health, the local church begins to see herself through the eyes of the Lord. Then and only then, through the healed and delivered individual members of the whole Church body will the world finally be able to see the beauty of, and in, the Church through the glorious beauty of our Lord Jesus Christ – our Bridegroom; our Healer.

Chapter Summary

- We can't reject people or healing through communion.

- We can't neglect to speak and declare the word of God

- We must maintain all efforts to maintain our healing

- We must rest in the victory we have over our enemies

DETERMINATION: God has given us the gift of healing; the abilities to heal and be healed so that we can manifest the healing of the nations. It is our duty as the Bride of Christ.

Church Work Book

Each question has several multiple-choice statements. Rate each statement with an answer from 1-5. "1" = not at all; "5" = frequently. Add your answers and find the results on page 144.

1. **Does your Church receive the healing elements?**
   a. The Sacraments are Jesus' body and blood
   b. Communion must not be partaken lightly
   c. Communion is a memorial until His return
   d. Communion represents Jesus' finished work

2. **Does your Church speak the Word of God?**
   a. We repeat the word each Sunday service
   b. We read the word out loud each week
   c. The Word is a part of our daily routine
   d. The Word of God is always in our mouths!

3. **Can your Church keep a healing culture?**
   a. We address healing as it is necessary
   b. We pray for healing on a regular basis
   c. We seek God for healing at every service
   d. We make healing a part of our daily lives!

4. **Can your whole Church be whole?**
   a. Our leadership is resistant to healing
   b. Our members are resistant to healing
   c. Leaders and members desire more healing
   d. We seek healing for our whole community!

Note: Each section has a possible rating ratio of 4-20 pts
Each chapter lesson has a possible rating ratio of 16-80 pts

Notes

_____

_____

_____

_____

_____

_____

_____

_____

_____

_____

_____

_____

_____

_____

Church Work Book Results

All workbook questions and their comments associated with the results are intended to be light-hearted ways to inspire change, encourage progress or illuminate areas of potential concern.

They are not to be considered as definitive, final or specifically accurate in their determinations. Nor are they meant to be offensive to your church's doctrine, beliefs or love of the Lord.

It is my prayer that you, your church and its leaders will walk in health, wholeness and the fullness of all that Jesus has provided for us through His death and resurrection, so that the whole Church of Jesus would walk in His Kingdom power and Glory.

CHAPTER 1; LESSON 1 – Calculate your points:
(Page 14)

1. Is your church living or dying?
    a. 4 points: Your church is just born or dying!
    b. 5-9 points: Your church is suffering!
    c. 10-14 points: Your church has potential!
    d. 15-20 points: Yay! Your church has life!
2. Is your church maturing?
    a. 4 points: Your church may not be growing!
    b. 5-9 points: Your church may be very young.
    c. 10-14 points: Your church is an adolescent.
    d. 15-20 points: Your church keeps maturing.
3. Is your church "normal?"
    a. 4 points: Yes, your people are like the world
    b. 5-9 points: Your church is like many others
    c. 10-14 points: Your church has a little mix
    d. 15-20 points: No, you look like the Word!
4. Does your church have symptoms of being sick?
    a. 4 points: Yes, it's time for an examination!
    b. 5-9 points: Maybe, so get a get a check-up!
    c. 10-14 points: A few, and easily remedied!
    d. 15-20 points: Minor, but you can be whole!

Total Synopsis – Chapter 1:
1. **16-25 points**: There is no new life coming in or being sustained by the church culture or teachings
2. **26-45 points:** There are definite warning signs that it may be time to consider making some changes
3. **46-65 points:** You are moving in the right direction, but there is still more work to get full church health
4. **66-80 points:** Your church has a life that people are drawn to, but make sure they have reason to stay and stay healthy! The pastor sets church example!

CHAPTER 2; LESSON 2 – Calculate your points:
(Page 26)

1. Does 1+1+1 mean to your Church?
   a. 4 pts: They have basic math skills.
   b. 5-9 pts: They understand "new math!"
   c. 10-14 pts: They have passed "calculous!"
   d. 15-20 pts: Yay! They're mathematicians!
2. What does your Church teach?
   a. 4 pts: They wonder why God uses sickness.
   b. 5-9 pts: They wonder when God will heal.
   c. 10-14 pts: They wonder why more aren't healed
   d. 15-20 pts: They wonder at God's power!
3. Does your church need the Word?
   a. 4 pts: Yes, and they need a whole lot more!
   b. 5-9 pts: Yes, but they still need a bit more.
   c. 10-14 pts: Yes, but they can handle more!
   d. 15-20 pts: They are getting it and more!
4. Is your church The Church?
   e. 4 pts: Maybe your Church attends church.
   f. 5-9 pts: Your Church has church services.
   g. 10-14 pts: Your Church is doing church work
   h. 15-20 pts: Your Church is being the Church!

Total Synopsis – Chapter 2:
1. **16-25 points**: Your Church may be lacking in an understanding of all God has for His people.
2. **26-45 points:** Your Church has a hope for what God can do, but may not know how to walk in His Word.
3. **46-65 points:** Your Church is moving in the right direction and as faith increases so will His power!
4. **66-80 points:** Your Church has a solid belief in what God wants to do in you and through you. The more you receive, the more you'll do for His Kingdom!

CHAPTER 3; LESSON 3 – Calculate your points:
(Page 44)

1. Is your church prevailing?
   a. 4 pts: They are being prevailed against.
   b. 5-9 pts: There is hope to begin prevailing.
   c. 10-14 pts: They are standing firm & strong!
   d. 15-20 pts: They are prevailing against hell!
2. Is your church like Jesus?
   a. 4 pts: They are having church for Jesus.
   b. 5-9 pts: They have compassion like Jesus.
   c. 10-14 pts: They have the power of Jesus!
   d. 15-20 pts: They do the works of Jesus!
3. Does your church believe the Truth?
   a. 4 pts: Yes, but maybe not all of His Truth.
   b. 5-9 pts: Yes, much of His Truth!
   c. 10-14 pts: Yes, the majority of His Truth.
   d. 15-20 pts: Yes, more and more of His Truth!
4. Is your church falling sick?
   a. 4 pts: Your Church may not be very healthy
   b. 5-9 pts: Your Church gets easily sick
   c. 10-14 pts: Your Church is walking in health
   d. 15-20 pts: Your Church heals & gets healed!

Total Synopsis – Chapter 3:
1. **16-25 points**: Your Church needs to know that Jesus has provided so much more for their lives.
2. **26-45 points:** Your Church has the potential for a "Truth Revival" from more knowledge of the Word.
3. **46-65 points:** Your Church believes God for His blessings but can still walk in more of His fullness!
4. **66-80 points:** Your Church believes in the healing power of Jesus for the His people today. Continue in truth and you'll manifest even greater power for the Kingdom of God in this dark and hurting world.

CHAPTER 4; LESSON 4 – Calculate your points:
(Page 71)

1. Does your church administer the Word?
    a. 4 pts: They may only be teaching traditions.
    b. 5-9 pts: They might only preach the Word.
    c. 10-14 pts: They are teaching and preaching.
    d. 15-20 pts: They are ministering the Word!
2. Is your church secretly suffering?
    a. 4 pts: There are probably unknown issues.
    b. 5-9 pts: Issues are known but unresolved.
    c. 10-14 pts: The issues are being prayed for.
    d. 15-20 pts: Issues are frequently healed!
3. Can your church be healed?
    a. 4 pts: Yes, but with a lot of re-training.
    b. 5-9 pts: Yes, but with a bit more re-thinking.
    c. 10-14 pts: Yes, with a little more believing.
    d. 15-20 pts: Yes, just a little more declaring!
4. Can your leaders make a difference?
    a. 4 pts: Yes, but with more understanding.
    b. 5-9 pts: Yes, with more personal revelation.
    c. 10-14 pts: Yes, with a little restructuring.
    d. 15-20 pts: Yes, and outside the church too!

Total Synopsis – Chapter 4:
1. **16-25 points:** Your Church only needs to trust in the Word more than solutions provided by the world.
2. **26-45 points:** Your Church knows that the prayers of the righteous can avail much and prays with hope.
3. **46-65 points:** Your Church is beginning to see that our faith can make us whole, but may struggle with faith.
4. **66-80 points:** Your Church knows that God's word provides real healing in their lives and the lives of others. Continue to trust that your Church can do greater works than Jesus[81] and boldly keep at it!

CHAPTER 5; LESSON 5 – Calculate your points:
(Page 95)

1. Is your church prepared for healing?
    a. 4 pts: They are surprised if there is healing.
    b. 5-9 pts: At times, they hope to see healing.
    c. 10-14 pts: They expect to see healings.
    d. 15-20 pts: They frequently see healings!
2. Is your church equipped to heal?
    a. 4 pts: They say healing is entirely up to God.
    b. 5-9 pts: They ask, hoping God will answer.
    c. 10-14 pts: They ask, believing to receive.
    d. 15-20 pts: They tell sickness what to do!
3. Is your church committed to change?
    a. 4 pts: They may not see a need for change.
    b. 5-9 pts: They think change will be difficult.
    c. 10-14 pts: They know change is needed.
    d. 15-20 pts: They look forward to new things!
4. Is your church contagious?
    a. 4 pts: Their beliefs aren't different at all.
    b. 5-9 pts: They have a desire to be different.
    c. 10-14 pts: They have started to be different.
    d. 15-20 pts: They set the trends for different!

Total Synopsis – Chapter 5:
1. **16-25 points**: Your Church might feel that supernatural healing is frightening. But just trust God and fear not!
2. **26-45 points:** Your Church has a hope for healing but may need to turn that hope towards faith in the Word!
3. **46-65 points:** Your Church expects God to do great things but they can do greater things through Jesus!
4. **66-80 points:** Your Church is continuing in the greater works assigned to them through the Word to destroy the works of the enemy! Keep seeking His will and you will be that light of a city on a hill that all will come to!

CHAPTER 6; LESSON 6 – Calculate your points:
(Page 116)

1. Will your Church survive?
    a. 4 pts: They may only be holding on to life.
    b. 5-9 pts: They are learning survival skills.
    c. 10-14 pts: They are experienced survivalists.
    d. 15-20 pts: They are pioneers in healing!
2. Will your Church thrive?
    a. 4 pts: They are satisfied to be content.
    b. 5-9 pts: They realize there is so much more.
    c. 10-14 pts: They have a holy discontent!
    d. 15-20 pts: They are reaching for God's best!
3. Will your Church bear fruit?
    a. 4 pts: Maybe not without some replanting.
    b. 5-9 pts: Yes, but only if carried away.
    c. 10-14 pts: Yes, with just a little pruning.
    d. 15-20 pts: Yes, and the harvest is abundant!
4. Will your Church overflow?
    a. 4 pts: Not if their cup stays half empty.
    b. 5-9 pts: Maybe. Their cup is half full.
    c. 10-14 pts: Yes, their cup is running over.
    d. 15-20 pts: Yes, exceedingly more and more!

Total Synopsis – Chapter 6:
1. **16-25 points**: Your Church may not even realize they are struggling to stay alive – spiritually and physically.
2. **26-45 points:** Your Church is desperate for the healing touch of God. Be encouraged knowing healing is yours.
3. **46-65 points:** Your Church knows healing is for you but may not know how to receive with unshakeable faith!
4. **66-80 points:** Your Church knows that healing is in our power! As you continue to grow in faith and boldness you will see healing throughout your church and city and serve as an example for other churches as well!

CHAPTER 7; LESSON 7 – Calculate your points:
(Page 135)

1. Can your Church receive healing through communion?
   a. 4 pts: Not without radical changes in beliefs
   b. 5-9 pts: Maybe, but only with serious changes
   c. 10-14 pts: Yes, with a few changes in beliefs
   d. 15-20 pts: Yes, and they probably already are!
2. Does your Church speak the Word of God?
   a. 4 pts: Probably not from a heart of belief
   b. 5-9 pts: Maybe, but without full understanding
   c. 10-14 pts: Yes, but possibly not enough
   d. 15-20 pts: Yes, and probably with bold faith!
3. Can your Church keep a healing culture?
   a. 4 pts: It will probably be difficult to start one
   b. 5-9 pts: Maybe, but with consistent leadership
   c. 10-14 pts: Yes, with diligence and faithfulness
   d. 15-20 pts: Yes, and they probably already do!
4. Can your whole Church be whole?
   a. 4 pts: YES, but with a lot of difficult work.
   b. 5-9 pts: YES, but it will be challenging.
   c. 10-14 pts: YES, just keep at it and don't give up!
   d. 15-20 pts: YES, and they are well on their way!

Total Synopsis – Chapter 7:
1. **16-25 points**: Your Church is missing out on the Glory of the Lord being expressed through their healing.
2. **26-45 points:** Your Church is hoping that the Glory of the Lord can still be expressed through their healing.
3. **46-65 points:** Your Church is praying and asking for the Glory of the Lord to be expressed through healing.
4. **66-80 points:** Your Church sees the Glory of the Lord being expressed through the healing and wholeness of its members. You can be the example to lead churches who are missing, hoping or praying for healing as well.

ENDNOTES

Endnotes Continued:

Endnotes Continued:

48. Matthew 13:58 - Because of their unbelief... .... pg. 84

49. Mark 9:29 – But by prayer and fasting .... pg. 84

50. Revelation 22:2 – Healing the Nations.......... .... pg. 93

51. Psalm 133:2 – Oil down Aaron's Beard .... pg. 93

52. Galatians 3:13/Psalm 107:2 – "I am Redeemed," .... pg. 98

53. Romans 8:28 – The Called according to purpose .... pg. 99

54. 3 John 1:2 – Prosperity: Health and Soul .... pg. 99

55. Amos 3:3 – How can two walk together .... pg. 102

56. Luke 6:45 – Out of the abundance of the heart......... pg. 103

57. James 3:11 – Sweet and bitter water........... .... pg. 103

58. 2 Corinthians 1:20 – All promises are yes! ... . Pg. 105

59. Mark 11:25 – Stand praying in forgiveness... .... pg. 106

60. Acts 2:43 & 47 – Increase to the church daily............ pg. 108

61. John 4:10 – Jesus Living Water......... .... pg. 108

62. Ephesians 5:26 – The Water of the Word pg.108

63. Galatians 5:22 – Fruit of the Spirit.... .... pg. 110

64. 3 John 1:2 – Prosperity & Health...... .... pg. 112

65. John 13:35 – Disciples who love Jesus .... pg. 115

66. Hebrews 6:14 – Blessed to be a blessing .... pg. 115

67. 1 Corinthians 15:26 – Death, the last enemy .... pg. 122

68. Psalm 107:20 – God sent His Word to Heal .. .. pg. 122

69. 1 Peter 2:24 – With His stripes we are healed........... pg. 122

70. Joel 3:10 – Let the weak say I am strong....... .... pg. 122

71. Genesis 6:3 – God's Spirit strives 120 years.. .... pg. 122

Endnotes Continued:

72. Deuteronomy 34:7 – Moses' eyes not dim ... . pg. 122

73. Revelation 22:2 – Healing the Nations .... pg. 127

74. John 1:12 – "Power" = Exousia: our authority .... pg. 130

75. Genesis 1:28 – Our God-given dominion .... pg. 130

76. Ephesians 3:12 – Speak boldly in faith .... pg. 130

77. Luke 10:19 – Power over the enemy's power............ pg. 130

78. Philippians 2:9 – Name above every name ... . pg. 130

79. 1 Corinthians 15:25 – Enemy prostrate at feet .... pg. 131

80. Ephesians 5:27 – Church without spot or blemish..... pg. 134

81. John 14:12 - Greater works than Jesus .... pg. 141

Image #1 - Taken from:
http://www.medcentral.org/Main/Whatssoimportantaboutcrawling.aspx
by Heather Haring, MedCentral Pediatric Therapist

Another important piece of development that occurs during the crawling stage is binocular vision. This involves training the eyes to look off into the distance and then back at the hands while crawling. Binocular vision is used when a child needs to copy something from a blackboard at school. Crawling is also a cross lateral movement that strengthens both the left and right side of the brain, allowing increased communication between the two sides of the brain and enhancing learning.

There is an interesting theory about a link between lack of crawling and attention-deficit/hyperactivity disorder. It all has to do with a reflex we are born with called the "symmetric tonic neck reflex" (STNR). This reflex helps us operate our upper and lower body independently. Usually this reflex is inhibited, or matures, between nine and twelve months. When a child gains independent control of his or her neck, arms and legs, the STNR is matured. This can be achieved through alternate hands and knees crawling for at least six months. When this reflex does not integrate, some of the symptoms are:

Tendency to slump when sitting at a desk
Difficulty keeping bottom in seat and feet on the floor when sitting at a desk
Poor eye-hand coordination
Slowness at copying tasks
Difficulty copying from a blackboard while at a desk
Difficulty with vertical tracking (important for math equations)
Poor attention
Clumsiness

The book "Stopping ADHD" cites a study by Dr. Miriam Bender that found that at least 75 percent of the learning-disabled people surveyed had an immature symmetric tonic neck reflex contributing to their disability.

Image #2 – Taken from:

https://www.mayoclinic.org/diseases-conditions/toe-walking/symptoms

Walking on the toes or the balls of the feet, also known as toe walking, is fairly common in children who are just beginning to walk. Most children outgrow it.

Kids who continue toe walking beyond the toddler years often do so out of habit. As long as your child is growing and developing normally, toe walking is unlikely to be a cause for concern.

Toe walking sometimes can result from certain conditions, including cerebral palsy, muscular dystrophy and autism spectrum disorder.

Symptoms

Toe walking is walking on the toes or the ball of the foot.

When to see a doctor

If your child is still toe walking after age 2, talk to your doctor about it. Make an appointment sooner if your child also has tight leg muscles, stiffness in the Achilles tendon or a lack of muscle coordination.

Causes

Typically, toe walking is a habit that develops when a child learns to walk. In a few cases, toe walking is caused by an underlying condition, such as:

- **A short Achilles tendon.** This tendon links the lower leg muscles to the back of the heel bone. If it's too short, it can prevent the heel from touching the ground.

Image #3 – Taken from:

https://www.asha.org/public/speech/disorders/adultSandL/
American Speech, Hearing and Language Association

Adult Speech and Language

There are many reasons why you might have a speech or language problem. Some problems start in childhood. Others happen after an illness or injury. Speech-language pathologists, or SLPs, can help.

Find out more about adult speech and language…

Speech Disorders

- Apraxia
- Dysarthria
- Stuttering
- Voice

Language Disorders

- Aphasia

Jesus...

"That he might present it to himself a glorious church, not having spot, or wrinkle, or any such thing; but that it should be holy and without blemish."
- Ephesians 5:27

May ALL of God's blessings be yours,
~Pastor Deidre Campbell-Jones

The House of His Glory

iChurch4Life

The House of His Glory is a Kingdom, Power and Glory congregation that believes church is not a place to go or a thing to have, but that The Church is who we are: A Church doing great and greater works for the Kingdom of Heaven; with the power of Jesus Christ and to the Glory of God!

You are invited to join this ministry and learn to walk in the fullness of all God has purposed you to do; have all that Jesus died on the cross for you to have and be exactly who God created you to be – the Church of Jesus Christ, His Bride, to be presented to Him without spot or blemish upon the day of His soon coming return.

Visit Pastor Deidre and The House of His Glory eChurch through "Ministries" at http://www.iChurch4Life.com. Also, you can download the "ichurch4life" App available for Smartphones on Google Play and the Apple Store.

Contact us for leadership training and resources, or to associate with or establish a ministry under the covering of Bishop Jason L. Sample and Pastor Deidre Jones.

Power, Love & Peace –
~Pastor Deidre Campbell-Jones, M.Th

www.ingramcontent.com/pod-product-compliance
Lightning Source LLC
LaVergne TN
LVHW011201080426
835508LV00007B/532